So You think you know HARRY POTTER ?

Clive Gifford

Question: What is the title of the Harry Potter book called in England, where author J.K. Rowling lives?

Answer: *Harry Potter and the Philosopher's Stone.*

Sometimes books have different titles, depending upon which country they're published in. So, for American readers, when you see mention of *Harry Potter and the Philosopher's Stone*, the questions (and answers) relate to the book known in the U.S. as *Harry Potter and the Sorcerer's Stone*.

Have fun!

© Copyright Hodder & Stoughton Ltd 2002

Published in 2002 for WH Smith,
Greenbridge Road, Swindon, SN3 3LD
by Hodder Children's Books

Editor: Isabel Thurston
Design by Fiona Webb
Cover design: Hodder Children's Books

The right of Clive Gifford to be identified as the author of the work has been asserted by him in accordance with the Copyright, Designs and Patents Act 1998.

20 19 18 17 16 15 14 13 12 11 10

ISBN: 034087337X

Printed by Bookmarque Ltd, Croydon, Surrey

Hodder Children's Books
a division of Hodder Headline Limited
338 Euston Road
London NW1 3BH

Contents

Introduction

So you think you know all about Harry Potter, his friends, enemies and fabulous adventures? This book is the ultimate test, as tough as making one of Professor Snape's potions and as slippery as a member of the Malfoy family. There are 300 questions devoted to each of the first four Harry Potter books – that's a whopping 1200 questions in total. This should keep you busy longer than it takes Hermione to write one of her eighteen-foot-long essays.

The questions for each book are divided into three levels of difficulty, shown by a star rating at the top of each page – one star ✪ for easy questions, two stars ✪✪ for medium and three ✪✪✪ for hard questions. If you can answer most of the questions in the hardest category without looking at the answers in the back of the book, then you're a true Harry Potter fan!

Who knows Harry Potter best?

Get together with your friends for a Harry Potter quiz challenge!

Nominate one friend to be chief quiz wizard. He or she picks questions for each player and awards house points for correct answers as follows: **easy** questions, one house point; **medium** questions, two house points; **hard** questions, three house points. Make sure that each player gets the same number of questions from each section.

Have fun!

Questions about Harry Potter and the Philosopher's Stone

1. What comes with a packet of Chocolate Frogs: a picture card, a toy or a free spell?

2. On which floor of Hogwarts was the forbidden corridor?

3. What is the surname of Harry's aunt and uncle, with whom he lives?

4. Who was awarded the ten house points that won Gryffindor the House Championship?

5. What bronze wizard coin begins with the letter K?

6. What sort of hat did Professor Quirrell wear in class?

7. Is Harry Potter left- or right-handed?

8. What did Ron's mother make Harry for Christmas?

9. Was Mrs Dursley putting out the cat, the dog or milk bottles when she discovered baby Harry on the doorstep?

10. In what sort of room did potions lessons take place: kitchens, laboratories or dungeons?

11. What creature is displayed on the Slytherin banner?

12. What is the name of the train that takes Harry from his home to the wizard's school?

13. What can the Philosopher's Stone turn any metal into?

14. How old is Harry when he is summoned to Hogwarts?

15. What colour pointed hat do first-year Hogwarts students wear?

16. Will the smallest or largest bottle get Harry through the black flames towards the Philosopher's Stone?

17. How did Harry's parents die, according to Mr and Mrs Dursley?

18. Is Nicolas Flamel over 400, over 600, over 800 or over 1000 years old?

19. What is the first name of Harry's uncle, Mr Dursley?

20. What colour is unicorn blood?

21. Is Professor Flitwick short, tall or very fat?

22. What instrument do Harry and his friends play to get past Fluffy?

23. Common Welsh Green and Hebridean Blacks are types of what creature?

24. From which train station does the Hogwarts Express leave?

25. Where did Harry spend Christmas: at the Dursleys', in Romania or at Hogwarts?

26. Which ball in Quidditch has two tiny silver wings?

27. What object produces the Elixir of Life?

28. At which platform would you find the Hogwarts Express arriving and departing?

29. Who owns a creature called Fluffy?

30. Which of Harry's parents did Lord Voldemort kill first?

31. In which Hogwarts house would you find Blaise Zabini and Draco Malfoy?

32. How many players are there in a Quidditch team?

33. In which street would you find the shop Flourish and Blotts?

34. Which team scored first in the Gryffindor v Slytherin Quidditch match?

35. Who was found underneath Professor Quirrell's headgear?

36. Who owned the Invisibility Cloak before Harry?

37. Which member of staff joined Harry's friends in the Quidditch stands?

38. Who owned a cat called Mrs Norris?

39. Vault 713 has no keyhole: true or false?

40. Who did Harry see reflected in the magical mirror with the gold frame?

41. What sort of creature is Peeves: a goblin, a Dementor or a poltergeist?

42. What happens in Quidditch when the golden snitch is caught?

43. Who is the caretaker at Hogwarts?

44. Who was the first in Harry's class to perform a *Wingardium Leviosa* spell correctly?

45. Sir Nicholas de Mimsy-Porpington is known by what nickname?

46. How tall was the troll found on Hallowe'en: six feet, ten feet, twelve feet or sixteen feet?

47. What sort of broomstick was Harry's first model?

48. Which Hogwarts student has a pet called Trevor?

49. Which girl joins Ron and Harry on their way to the duel with Malfoy?

50. What did Flamel and Dumbledore agree to do with the Philosopher's Stone?

51. How many house points had Harry collected from Gryffindor in his first week: minus three, minus two, two or three?

52. What colour is the Slytherin Quidditch kit?

53. Charlie Weasley works with dragons in which country: Romania, Bulgaria or Slovenia?

54. Which of the Weasleys did not have a letter knitted into their new jumper?

55. Against which house was Harry's first Quidditch match?

56. What is the name of Ron's pet rat?

57. How many Chasers do you find on a Quidditch team?

58. Where did Harry sleep in the Dursleys' house for more than ten years?

59. Who did Hermione and Ron think jinxed Harry's broom during his first game of Quidditch?

60. Who invented Every Flavour Beans?

61. Is a Quaffle the size of a golf ball, cricket ball or soccer ball?

62. How many houses are there at Hogwarts?

63. What type of creatures are Ronan and Bane?

64. Who becomes the youngest house Quidditch player in a century?

65. Which Hogwarts house does Harry hope not to be placed in?

66. What is the first name of Harry's aunt, Mrs Dursley?

67. Which Hogwarts house was the Fat Friar ghost in when alive?

68. In which room at Hogwarts are meals served?

69. What sort of object is the Comet Two Sixty?

70. Lord Voldemort created the Philosopher's Stone: true or false?

71. What colour hair does Ron Weasley have?

72. Hagrid bent Uncle Vernon's rifle into a knot: true or false?

73. What creature has Hagrid always wanted?

74. What colour were Lord Voldemort's eyes?

75. Was Professor Binns a centaur, a ghost or a werewolf?

76. What part of Harry's head hurt after he saw the cloaked figure in the Forbidden Forest?

77. What game, in a giant version, bars Harry and his friends' way to the Philosopher's Stone?

78. On which date does the Hogwarts school year start: 1 August, 1 September or 1 October?

79. For which house did Angelina Johnson play Chaser?

80. Which team won the final Quidditch match of the year: Ravenclaw or Gryffindor?

81. Whose wand was the first to send up red sparks in the Forbidden Forest: Draco's, Neville's, Harry's or Ron's?

82. Is the Leaky Cauldron a wizarding repair shop, a pub or a café?

83. What number is the Dursleys' house on Privet Drive?

84. Which member of the Weasley family is a Hogwarts prefect?

85. Which fellow Hogwarts student did Harry chase up into the sky in his first flying lesson?

86. Who is known as You-Know-Who?

87. Who came top of Harry's year in the exams?

88. What colour is Harry Potter's hair?

89. What colour is a Sickle coin?

90. What position is Harry to play in Quidditch?

91. Who brought baby Harry to the Dursleys' house on a motorbike?

92. On what train does Harry first talk to Ron?

93. Who does Harry meet in the last chamber?

94. Who sold the wand that created the scar on Harry's head?

95. Who killed the Bones, the Prewetts and the McKinnons?

96. Is dragon breeding illegal or legal?

97. What is the name of the street on which Harry and the Dursleys live?

98. Where are Harry and the others to do their detention?

99. What shape is Harry's special scar?

100. Who saved Harry in the last chamber?

101. What does Hagrid buy Harry as an eleventh birthday present?

102. Who set Professor Snape's robes on fire?

103. Name two members of Dudley Dursley's four-boy gang?

104. At which pub did Hagrid win the dragon's egg: the Three Broomsticks, the Hog's Head or the Leaky Cauldron?

105. What subject does Professor Binns teach?

106. How many of Ron's brothers went to Hogwarts before him?

107. What was contained inside the big leather book that Hagrid gave to Harry?

108. What magical device are first-years not usually allowed at Hogwarts?

109. What chess piece does Ron play against Professor McGonagall's giant pieces?

110. Who comes to collect Harry Potter and take him to Hogwarts?

111. Which teacher refereed the second Quidditch match Harry played in?

112. What was the first name of Harry's mother?

113. How many ways did Professor Dumbledore discover of using dragon's blood?

114. Who is the resident ghost of Gryffindor house?

115. What do Harry and Draco see the cloaked figure do to the unicorn?

116. Can you name any two of the three creatures that Hogwarts first-years are allowed to own?

117. Which school's uniform included orange knickerbockers and a straw hat?

118. What position did Ron Weasley's brother, Bill, once hold at Hogwarts?

119. What colour was the key Harry caught whilst riding the broomstick?

120. What was the name of the device Dumbledore used to switch the street lights off in Privet Drive?

121. Which Professor announced that there was a troll in the dungeons, before fainting?

122. Where would you find Eeylops Owl Emporium?

123. How many house points did Slytherin finish the year on: 397, 463, 472 or 497?

124. What are rumoured to guard the vaults of Gringott's bank?

125. Who taught Harry's first flying lesson?

126. Who foiled Harry's early-rising plan to get the third letter sent to him at the Dursleys?

127. What does Professor Flitwick stand on when giving lessons?

128. Who performs a door-unlocking spell to get into the forbidden corridor?

129. Which item is not required kit for first-year students at Hogwarts: wand, set of brass scales, microscope or cauldron?

130. In which Hogwarts house would you find Millicent Bulstrode?

131. What did Hagrid give Harry as a Christmas present?

132. How many Knuts to a Sickle: 29, 33, 39 or 43?

133. What happened to Hagrid's wand when he was expelled?

134. What does drinking the Elixir of Life do to a person?

135. Which bank does Bill Weasley work for?

136. What is a Muggle?

137. Which Quidditch position did Terence Higgs play for Slytherin?

138. What is the name of the shop in Diagon Alley that sells wizarding robes?

139. Who received a video camera, a remote-control aeroplane, a cine-camera and sixteen new computer games for one birthday?

140. In which continent does Bill Weasley work?

141. In which year did Dumbledore defeat Grindelwald: 1745, 1825, 1925 or 1945?

142. How long did Harry's second game of Quidditch last: five minutes, fifteen minutes, five hours or five days?

143. How many hands does Dumbledore's golden watch have?

144. Where did Ron end up after being bitten by Hagrid's dragon?

145. No two wands from Ollivanders are the same: true or false?

146. What happens when Harry opens a book from the Restricted Section of the library?

147. What was the first name of Harry's father?

148. What is Neville searching for the first time he meets Harry?

149. The Weasleys' parents were in which house at Hogwarts?

150. What pub stands between a bookshop and a record shop?

151. What type of hat is the Sorting Hat?

152. What did Hagrid do on the train to London: sleep, sing, read or knit?

153. Who is the resident ghost of Slytherin house?

154. What magical present did Harry receive at Christmas?

155. Which two students always accompanied Draco Malfoy?

156. What colour playing pieces do Harry and his friends play to get to the Philosopher's Stone?

157. How many Sickle coins make a Galleon:
7, 14, 17 or 21?

158. Inside what object did the 24 letters
addressed to Harry arrive?

159. How many staircases are there at
Hogwarts: 72, 92, 142 or 192?

160. As what creature did Professor
McGonagall first arrive at the Dursleys'
house?

161. What is the name of Hagrid's dog?

162. What street lies behind the Leaky
Cauldron?

163. What position does Professor
McGonagall hold at Hogwarts?

164. Which member of the Weasley family
was Captain of Quidditch?

165. Who lied about the troll to save Ron and
Harry from a telling-off?

166. What can one buy at the shop Flourish
and Blotts?

167. Who does Firenze think killed the unicorn?

168. What was the name of Uncle Vernon's old school?

169. Which team scored 170 points in Harry's first Quidditch match?

170. Who reached the rock in the sea to take Harry to Hogwarts?

171. Who looked after the Invisibility Cloak and eventually gave it to Harry?

172. Griphook can be found working in what place?

173. What was the only thing Hermione ever lost at?

174. How many times had Harry been to London before Hagrid took him?

175. Is a Remembrall: a memory aid, a language translator or a wizard's pocket calculator?

176. Who was a partner of Dumbledore, has a wife called Perenelle and made the Philosopher's Stone?

177. What is Professor Dumbledore's favourite sport: cricket, ten pin bowling or lacrosse?

178. Whose friends were going to take Hagrid's dragon to Romania?

179. What is the name of Dudley Dursley's best friend?

180. What subject does Professor Flitwick teach at Hogwarts?

181. In which room did Ron and Harry lock the troll on Hallowe'en night?

182. Who first owned Scabbers the rat?

183. Is the Golden Snitch the size of a peanut, walnut, grapefruit or melon?

184. Who broke a leg and couldn't look after Harry on Dudley's birthday?

185. Does Professor Dumbledore like world music, chamber music, rock music or jazz?

186. What is the name of the centaur who gives Harry a ride on his back to get him out of danger?

187. Is a Galleon a gold, silver or bronze wizard coin?

188. Who was in the room with the mirror the third night Harry visited?

189. What weapon did Uncle Vernon face Hagrid with?

190. How many house points did Professor Dumbledore award Ron for his chess playing?

191. What are the Weasley twins called?

192. What newspaper for wizards does Hagrid read?

193. What object was the troll carrying on the night of the Hallowe'en feast?

194. How many sets of plain black robes are first-year Hogwarts students required to own?

195. How many bottles are involved in Professor Snape's test to reach the Philosopher's Stone?

196. What flavour cake did Hagrid give Harry for his eleventh birthday?

197. What are the two black balls in Quidditch called?

198. Monkshood and wolfsbane are two different plants: true or false?

199. What is the surname of the little girl called Ginny?

200. What type of Quidditch player gets injured most often?

201. How many house points did Professor Dumbledore award Harry for courage?

202. How many years has Slytherin won the House Championship in a row?

203. What creature's tentacles were the Weasley twins and Lee Jordan tickling after the exams?

204. What curse occurs when the words *Locomotor Mortis* are uttered?

205. What colour were the tailcoats worn at Smeltings School?

206. In the practical exams, what fruit did the students have to make tap-dance?

207. What is Professor Dumbledore's first name?

208. How many house points did Hermione lose for Gryffindor because of the troll?

209. Which student ran away when he saw the cloaked figure by the unicorn?

210. From what sort of wood is the handle of a Nimbus Two Thousand made?

211. Which professor's security spell wasn't a spell at all but a logic puzzle?

212. *Wingardium Leviosa* is a charm that does what to objects?

213. What sport is Dean Thomas's favourite?

214. Who is the keeper of the keys at Hogwarts?

215. How many different fouls are there in Quidditch?

216. Who saved Professor Snape's life many years ago?

217. Professor Dumbledore has a scar above his left knee in the shape of what map?

218. Who does Hermione perform a full Body-Bind spell on?

219. In which English county does Nicolas Flamel live?

220. What animal feature did Hagrid magically give Dudley Dursley?

221. What percentage did Professor Flitwick tell Hermione she got in her exam?

222. How many Galleons did Harry's wand cost from Ollivanders?

223. Who lost twenty house points for wandering about on the night Harry and his friends were trying to release the dragon?

224. What present did George and Fred Weasley try to send Harry when he was in the hospital wing?

225. Who was the referee at Harry's first Quidditch match?

226. What is the name of the company that Mr Dursley works for?

227. What were the three words on the note that came pinned to Harry's cloak when it was returned?

228. Who teaches herbology classes at Hogwarts?

229. Who performed a Leg-Locker curse on Neville?

230. Name one present Harry received for his tenth birthday?

231. In whose class did the students have to turn a mouse into a snuff-box?

232. Where are broomsticks kept when not in use?

233. Whose wand got stuck up the troll's nose on Hallowe'en night?

234. Who is the Minister for Magic?

235. What plant do Harry, Hermione and Ron land on after jumping through the trapdoor?

236. What is the name of the old lady with whom Harry usually spends Dudley's birthdays?

237. What spell was placed on the new quills especially for exams?

238. What sort of snake frightens the Dursleys on Dudley's birthday trip to the zoo?

239. What are the students serving detention supposed to do if they find the hurt unicorn?

240. What creature hurt Professor Snape's leg?

241. Who took away 150 house points from Gryffindor after Harry and the others were caught?

242. What building tool does the company that Mr Dursley works for make?

243. Where did Professors Snape and Quirrell meet so that they wouldn't be overheard?

244. Who describes Harry as a natural on a broomstick?

245. What sort of dragon is Hagrid's pet?

246. Who lent Hagrid the motorbike on which Harry Potter makes his first appearance?

247. What do Hermione Granger's parents do for a living?

248. Which professor was at school with Harry's father?

249. Where was Professor Dumbledore called to after the exams?

250. What is Professor McGonagall's first name?

251. How many broomsticks arrived to take the dragon away from Hogwarts?

252. How many letters were sent to Harry the day after he was sent twelve?

253. What is the name of the three-headed dog guarding the trapdoor?

254. In what month was Harry's first Quidditch match?

255. What sort of creature is half-man and half-horse?

256. Who does Harry pretend he and his friends are, to make Peeves leave them alone?

257. What item is Harry surprised to see in the last chamber?

258. What does the Mirror of Erised show to a person?

259. With what animal's blood, along with brandy, do you feed a baby dragon?

260. What object knocked the troll out?

261. Which local comprehensive school was Harry due to go to?

262. What position in Quidditch do George and Fred Weasley play?

263. What colour eyes does Firenze have?

264. What was Harry's least favourite lesson of his first week at Hogwarts?

265. What did Professor Dumbledore tell Harry he saw when he looked into the Mirror of Erised?

266. What sort of creature works at Gringott's Wizarding Bank?

267. Who caught Harry, Hermione and Ron as they walked down the tower?

268. From what animal's stomach is a bezoar taken?

269. Name one of the two parts of a unicorn that Harry used in potion lessons?

270. What present did the Dursleys give Harry for Christmas?

271. Which Hogwarts student sacrifices himself to let Harry get closer to the Philosopher's Stone?

272. From what kind of wood was Harry's father's wand made?

273. What name did Hagrid give his baby dragon?

274. What is Professor Snape's first name?

275. What toy did Hagrid pack with his pet dragon to keep it company?

276. What unpleasant flavour bean did Professor Dumbledore eat by Harry's bedside?

277. Who does Malfoy say will be his second in the duel with Harry?

278. Which two students originally go with Fang into the Forbidden Forest?

279. Which Hogwarts house does Pansy Parkinson belong to?

280. What was written on the banner that Harry's friends held at the first Quidditch match?

281. What knocked-out creature did Harry walk past to head towards the Philosopher's Stone?

282. Who lent Harry his wizard's chess set for the Christmas holidays?

283. What was the first-years' last exam?

284. What kind of coins does Harry use to pay the owl that delivers Hagrid's newspaper?

285. Who did Ron see when he looked into the magical mirror?

286. Which friend of the Weasley twins commented on Quidditch matches?

287. From what material is a Remembrall made?

288. *Caput Draconis* is the password for what part of Hogwarts?

289. Where does Harry head for, the first time he uses his Invisibility Cloak?

290. Who is believed to be the only person Lord Voldemort is afraid of?

291. How many points are scored when the Quaffle goes through one of the hoops in Quidditch?

292. What time of day were Harry, his friends and Draco Malfoy to start their detention?

293. Who is captain of the Gryffindor Quidditch team?

294. Harry's mother's wand was made from wood from which tree?

295. What injury did Neville suffer during his first flying lesson?

296. To which hotel did Uncle Vernon take his family and Harry to escape the flow of letters for Harry?

297. At what time are Harry and Draco Malfoy supposed to have their wizards' duel?

298. Who confiscated *Quidditch Through The Ages* from Harry?

299. Who was Harry's partner in Charms class when they first made objects fly?

300. What subject does Professor McGonagall teach: Quidditch, Transfiguration or Divination?

Questions about Harry Potter and the Chamber of Secrets

1. Which creature sang a Valentine to Harry: a frog, a dwarf, or a cat?

2. What was the name of the tree Harry and Ron crashed the car into?

3. Who was the author of most of the books Harry needed for his second year at Hogwarts?

4. Which house at Hogwarts won the House Cup for the second year in a row?

5. How many goalposts are there on a Quidditch pitch?

6. Who, out of Lucius Malfoy, Arthur Weasley and Vernon Dursley, is a governor of Hogwarts school?

7. Which Hogwarts house turned out more dark wizards and witches than any other?

8. Which ghost haunts the girls' toilets on the first floor of Hogwarts?

9. What did Harry nearly forget to take with him as he escaped from the Dursleys'?

10. Which member of the Weasley family was taken into the Chamber of Secrets?

11. Was Hogwarts founded over 250 years, over 500 years, over 1000 years or over 2500 years ago?

12. Where are underage Wizards not allowed to use magic?

13. Which founder of Hogwarts was able to talk to snakes?

14. Who received a Howler letter from his mother?

15. How many people were found Petrified near the library at the time of a Quidditch match?

16. What sort of wizarding items are sold at Gambol and Japes?

17. Was Tom Riddle's mother a witch or a Muggle?

18. What is rumoured to be inside the Chamber of Secrets: great treasure, the Philosopher's Stone or a monster?

19. What is a really rude name for someone who is born to Muggles?

20. What is the name of the librarian at Hogwarts?

21. Which student was forced to act out many of Lockhart's adventures at the front of the class?

22. Is Colin Cheevey's father a policeman, a postman or a milkman?

23. Tears from phoenix birds have healing powers: true or false?

24. What place did Harry miss greatly in the summer holidays?

25. Into which part of Harry's body did the Basilisk fang inject poison?

26. Which of Harry's friends arrives at the Dursleys' first?

27. For how long was Hermione in the hospital wing: several hours, several days, several weeks or several months?

28. Who was believed to have built the Chamber of Secrets?

29. What happened to the end of year exams as a school treat?

30. Which house, apart from Gryffindor, had the Sorting Hat considered putting Harry in?

31. Where is Harry's trunk, containing his Hogwarts kit, stored at the Dursleys'?

32. How many people founded Hogwarts school?

33. Who invited Harry, Hermione and Ron to his Deathday party?

34. What colour was the diary that Harry and Ron discovered?

35. Fred bewitched Percy Weasley's prefect badge to read: peabrain, pinhead or puny?

36. Which ghost was gloomy as he had been barred from joining the Headless Hunters Club?

37. Who won *Witch Weekly*'s Most-Charming-Smile award five times in a row?

38. How many years ago was the Chamber of Secrets last opened: 20, 50, 70 or 100?

39. What creatures picked Harry and Ron up in the Forbidden Forest?

40. What sort of creature is Dobby?

41. Is Gilderoy Lockhart's book-signing in the morning, afternoon or evening?

42. Which ghost told Harry and Ron about the diary found in the girls' toilets?

43. Was Hagrid expelled from Hogwarts in his first year, second year, third year or fourth year?

44. Which member of the Weasley family is starting at Hogwarts for the first time?

45. What is the name of Harry's pet owl?

46. Which family's father has a boss called Cornelius Fudge?

47. What special powder do Harry and the Weasleys use to travel to Diagon Alley in the summer holidays?

48. Who, after receiving advice, chose all the same new subjects as Ron Weasley?

49. Is Professor Sprout a living wizard, a living witch or a ghost?

50. What did Harry receive from the Dursleys for his birthday: a card, money, a shirt or nothing?

51. What hair did Hermione put in her glass of Polyjuice Potion by mistake?

52. What did the car carrying Ron and Harry crash into: a greenhouse, the castle wall or a tree?

53. Aragog was the creature from the Chamber of Secrets: true or false?

54. Who sent Harry a singing Valentine?

55. What newspaper features a headline about Ron and Harry's journey in the flying car?

56. Which teacher uses a purple megaphone at the Gryffindor v Hufflepuff Quidditch match?

57. Between which two houses was the first Quidditch match of the season?

58. Who had to help Lockhart with his fan mail as a detention?

59. Which Hogwarts house is Ernie Macmillan in?

60. What plant, beginning with the letter M, is used in most antidotes to curses?

61. Penelope Clearwater was a first-year, a prefect or a Chaser at Quidditch?

62. Into which Hogwarts house was Colin Creevey sorted?

63. From what official body does Harry receive a warning in the summer holidays?

64. Which team in the first match of the season did most of the neutrals from other houses support?

65. Which place, beginning with A, is Hagrid going to be taken to as a precaution?

66. To get rid of a gnome you pick it up by the ankles and swing it round your head: true or false?

67. Who flew Mr Weasley's car to Hogwarts?

68. What Quidditch balls do the beaters try to keep away from their team?

69. During which holidays did second-years have to think about what subjects they would take in their third year?

70. What does George use to open Harry's locked bedroom door: a hairpin, an unlocking spell or a crowbar?

71. Tom Riddle was once Head Boy of Hogwarts: true or false?

72. Which member of the Weasleys started to read a book called *Prefects Who Gained Power*?

73. What colour moustache did Uncle Vernon have?

74. What comes to rescue Harry and Ron from the masses of spiders?

75. Which Hogwarts student's father is called Lucius?

76. Who do Ron and Harry force down the pipe towards the Chamber of Secrets?

77. Whose father works in the Misuse of Muggle Artefacts Office?

78. What day did Lockhart insist on the school celebrating as a morale-booster?

79. Who wrote *Year with a Yeti* and *Wanderings with Werewolves?*

80. Who did Riddle fight in the dungeons 50 years ago?

81. Who does Harry give his free copies of Lockhart's books to?

82. Was Tom Riddle's father a wizard or a muggle?

83. What position does Alicia Spinnet play at Quidditch?

84. What sort of exams does O.W.L. stand for?

85. What piece of clothing did Harry and Ron use to visit Hagrid without being spotted?

86. For which house team does Katie Bell play Quidditch?

87. Were Tom Riddle and Harry Potter both orphans?

88. Who stops letters reaching Harry in the summer holidays?

89. What object of Ron Weasley's was badly damaged in the car crash at Hogwarts?

90. Who had a rare laugh when mentioning Hermione had a tail?

91. Where is Harry told to stay during the Dursleys' dinner party?

92. Which Professor came to visit Hagrid's cabin moments after Ron and Harry arrived?

93. What feature does Hogwarts overlook: the sea, a lake or a mountain?

94. Who earns Gryffindor ten house points in their very first lesson back at Hogwarts?

95. How many governors of Hogwarts school are there: six, ten, twelve or eighteen?

96. Who comes with Ron to rescue Harry from the Dursleys?

97. Who had instructed Ginny Weasley to strangle the roosters and daub the scary messages?

98. What weapon magically appeared inside the Sorting Hat?

99. What sort of creature do the Weasleys have in their attic: a ghoul, a poltergeist, a house-elf or a dragon?

100. Which friend of Harry's was found Petrified near the library?

101. Tom Riddle was a first-year, third-year or fifth-year student when the Chamber of Secrets was opened?

102. Which ghost was teased by Olive Hornby when alive because of her glasses?

103. What chamber did the scary message written in foot-high letters on Hallowe'en refer to?

104. Mafalda Hopkirk works at Hogwarts, the Improper Use of Magic Office or the Leaky Cauldron?

105. Where do Ron and Hermione start work on the Polyjuice Potion?

106. How many years is it since Nearly Headless Nick died: 100, 250, 500 or 1000?

107. Who was found between the feet of the giant statue in the Chamber of Secrets?

108. What subject did Gilderoy Lockhart teach at Hogwarts?

109. What was the name in the diary found in the girls' toilets?

110. Which two fathers have a brawl in Flourish and Blotts?

111. Whose possessions were ransacked in the Gryffindor dormitory?

112. Into whose cauldron did Harry throw a firework during a potions lesson?

113. What sort of creature is Aragog?

114. Which teacher was unable to round up Cornish pixies with his wand?

115. What colour is Mr Weasley's car: green, turquoise, pink or purple?

116. What subject at Hogwarts is all about the world of non-wizards?

117. Who was sacked as a school governor after the events in the Chamber of Secrets?

118. What device does Uncle Vernon personally fit to Harry's bedroom door after the dinner party?

119. What item did Dobby fix to hurt Harry enough to make him leave Hogwarts?

120. Who is the Slytherin Quidditch team's new Seeker?

121. Who used *Expelliarmus* to force Riddle's diary to shoot out of Malfoy's hands?

122. Where did the Bludger hit Harry: his wrist, elbow, knee or head?

123. Is the new password to get into Gryffindor Tower: wafflebird, wattlebird, wafflefrog or wattlefowl?

124. How long do the effects of the Polyjuice Potion last?

125. Which founder of Hogwarts left the school?

126. What piece of furniture is the Sorting Hat placed on?

127. Which ghost appears to have a crush on Harry after his adventures in the Chamber of Secrets?

128. What creatures does Ron not like when they're alive?

129. What is the name of the creature Harry finds in his bedroom at the Dursleys'?

130. What sort of potion transforms a person into someone else?

131. What kept coming out of Ron's mouth after his spell aimed at Draco Malfoy backfired?

132. Do the two serpents carved on the stone door to the Chamber of Secrets have emeralds, rubies or diamonds for eyes?

133. What prize does Lockhart offer to the best poem about the Wagga Wagga Werewolf?

134. Who did Harry become to get into Slytherin house?

135. *The Standard Book of Spells, Grade 2* was written by Miranda Goshawk, Mirabelle Sparrowhawk or Mandy Blackhawk?

136. The Hogwarts Express first heads in which direction when leaving King's Cross station?

137. How does Professor Binns often enter his classroom: through the blackboard, through the door or through the ceiling?

138. Who called Hermione a 'Mudblood' on the Quidditch pitch?

139. Who stopped Harry going through the barrier to board the Hogwarts Express?

140. What type of bird flies in to deliver a letter at the Dursleys' dinner table?

141. What happened to Hermione's face after drinking Polyjuice Potion?

142. What object did the bird drop at Harry's feet in the Chamber of Secrets?

143. What colour is Mrs Norris the cat?

144. What weapon does Hagrid point at Ron and Harry when they come to visit?

145. In what street would you find Borgin and Burkes?

146. Who does Filch think harmed his cat, Mrs Norris, on Hallowe'en night?

147. What colour is the Quaffle?

148. What is the name of Dumbledore's pet bird?

149. What creature came out of the mouth of the statue in the Chamber of Secrets?

150. What creature is small, leathery and has a bald head like a potato?

151. Behind whose left ear did Harry spot the Golden Snitch?

152. What was the name of the correspondence course in magic for beginners Harry found in Filch's office?

153. Which two students missed the train to Hogwarts?

154. A Basilisk's stare can kill people: true or false?

155. Whose office is reached by a spiral staircase and the password 'Sherbet Lemon'?

156. What sort of creature are Errol and Hermes?

157. What object followed Harry throughout the first Quidditch match?

158. How many girls are there on the Slytherin Quidditch team: none, one, two or three?

159. What was found underneath the scary message written on Hallowe'en night?

160. Who is Harry paired with in Duelling Club?

161. What sort of flying broom does Ron have: a Comet 260, a Shooting Star or a Nimbus Two Thousand?

162. Who caught the Golden Snitch in the first Quidditch match of the season?

163. What is the first name of Ron's dad, Mr Weasley?

164. Whose get-well card did Hermione hide under her pillow?

165. What surprising object belonging to the Weasley family did Harry and Ron find in the Forbidden Forest?

166. Which Hogwarts student was Petrified on his way to visit Harry in the hospital wing?

167. Who supplies Ron and Harry with the new password into Gryffindor Tower?

168. Is *Rictusempra* a Tickling Charm, a curse that makes your legs move out of control or a Shrinking Spell?

169. Which Hogwarts teacher signs a note to let Hermione into the Restricted Section of the library?

170. Who repaired Harry's glasses with one tap of his wand?

171. Who did Harry set free from being a servant of the Malfoys?

172. Who do Ron and Harry follow to get into Slytherin house?

173. What colour envelope does a Howler letter come in?

174. What was Tom Riddle's middle name?

175. What important item of his did Harry break the first time he used Floo powder?

176. Which two teachers are in charge of second-year Duelling Club?

177. In which Hogwarts house is Justin Finch-Fletchley?

178. *Tarantallegra* is a spell that shrinks the victim to the size of a matchstick: true or false?

179. What did Harry and Ron spot in Hermione's clenched fist?

180. Which professor did *not* carry Justin Finch-Fletchley to the hospital wing: Flitwick, McGonagall or Sinistra?

181. From what newspaper was the photographer who took pictures of Harry and Gilderoy Lockhart?

182. Which ghost does Harry discover Petrified and smoky black in colour?

183. How many house points did Gryffindor lose as a result of Harry and Ron's journey in the flying car: ten, none, 25 or 50?

184. What creature, beginning with the letter B, is also known as the King of Serpents?

185. What Christmas present did Harry receive from Hermione?

186. In which Diagon Alley shop did Gilderoy Lockhart have a book signing session?

187. Is Aragog the size of a cat, the size of a dog or the size of an elephant?

188. What did Uncle Vernon do to the cage of Harry's pet owl in the summer holidays?

189. Which two Hogwarts students did Hermione manage to send to sleep?

190. Which tree in the grounds of Hogwarts grounds hits back at anything that hits it?

191. What creature does Hagrid say people should follow if they want to find out things?

192. Which Quidditch team has a set of its robes in the window of Quality Quidditch Supplies?

193. Which teacher does Harry accuse of running away?

194. What did Lucius Malfoy give each member of the Slytherin Quidditch team?

195. What part of Harry was bitten the first time he tried to de-gnome the Weasley's garden?

196. What bird enters the Chamber of Secrets to surprise Harry and Tom Riddle?

197. What did Harry get from the Dursleys for Christmas?

198. What creatures are around eight inches high, blue in colour and very naughty?

199. Which student has a girlfriend called Penelope Clearwater?

200. What sort of solution makes parts of your body expand in size?

201. What object does Harry force the Basilisk fang into?

202. What did Fred, George and Ron have to do as a punishment for flying their father's car?

203. What was the name of the liquid Harry had to take to bring back the bones in his arm?

204. Whose name is engraved into the sword Harry used in the Chamber of Secrets?

205. Who was the headmaster of Hogwarts 50 years ago?

206. How many times was Nearly Headless Nick hit in the neck with a blunt axe?

207. What does Dobby drop and smash at the Dursleys'?

208. Where did Harry and Ron hide in the staff room?

209. How many O.W.Ls is Percy Weasley taking?

210. What happened to the Gryffindor v Hufflepuff Quidditch match?

211. What make and model was Mr Weasley's car?

212. The sound of which creature can kill a Basilisk?

213. Who loses his wand and is thrown into a wall when demonstrating duelling?

214. What heals Harry from the poison of the Basilisk?

215. Which Hogwarts house was Penelope Clearwater in?

216. Which professors brought Colin Cheevey to Madam Pomfrey?

217. What is the name of the Weasley family's house?

218. Who wore an orange hat and a revolving bow tie at Nearly Headless Nick's party?

219. Who announces that Professor Dumbledore is to be suspended?

220. How many house points each do Ron and Harry earn from Dumbledore after their adventures?

221. Professor Sinistra is in which department at Hogwarts?

222. What was the surname of the rich builder visiting Mr and Mrs Dursley for an evening meal?

223. What do all the students wear when potting Mandrake plants?

224. Of what crime was Aragog falsely accused?

225. Which of the following items is *not* in the student store-cupboard: leeches, knotgrass, bicorn horn, fluxweed?

226. What happened to Harry's arm after Lockhart tried to mend the break?

227. How many four-poster beds are there in the Gryffindor second-year dormitory?

228. Who is the second Hogwarts student to be Petrified?

229. How old was Tom Riddle when he wrote his diary?

230. Who is Ron's favourite Quidditch team?

231. Which adult declares himself to be a Squib in front of teachers and some students?

232. What subject does Ron want to give up in his third year?

233. What did Hagrid give Harry for Christmas?

234. What type of broomstick are the Slytherin Quidditch team equipped with?

235. Which Hogwarts student bought a rotting newt-tail and a purple crystal to protect him from the Chamber of Secrets monster?

236. What item of clothing did Harry place the diary inside before handing it back to Lucius Malfoy?

237. Who tried to scrub the message written on Hallowe'en night but couldn't remove it?

238. How many Galleons was Arthur Weasley fined for bewitching a Muggle car?

239. What strange sight did Harry see when he stared at the Dursleys' hedge?

240. What is the only type of charm that Gilderoy Lockhart is any good at?

241. How had Professor Binns died?

242. What is Mrs Weasley's first name?

243. Which student was down to go to Eton before coming to Hogwarts?

244. Who fills in as head of Hogwarts after Dumbledore is suspended?

245. What sort of creature were shown to the class in their first Defence Against The Dark Arts lesson?

246. What sort of food did Hermione fill with a Sleeping Draught?

247. Professor Dippet's first name was: Alfredo, Armando or Alberto?

248. What was the first name of the Hogwarts founder, Ravenclaw?

249. What is the name of Gilderoy Lockhart's autobiography?

250. What password gets Harry and Ron into Slytherin house?

251. Who does Harry say gave Ginny Weasley the diary when they were in a wizard's bookshop?

252. Who sounds the alarm on finding Harry with two more Petrified victims?

253. What is a person born into a wizard family but without any magical powers called?

254. How many years did it take for Tom Riddle to discover everything about the Chamber of Secrets?

255. Who is Millicent Bulstrode's partner in Duelling Club?

256. What is the name for someone who can talk to snakes?

257. What potion did Madam Pomfrey use to help cure colds at Hogwarts?

258. What is the name of Hagrid's dog, which Ron and Harry take into the Forbidden Forest?

259. Whose hair did Hermione think she had for the Polyjuice Potion?

260. What plant was going to be used to revive Colin and Mrs Norris?

261. How many Galleons were in the Weasleys' vault at Gringotts?

262. What position did Lockhart say he played at Quidditch?

263. Who arrived from the Ministry of Magic to take Hagrid away?

264. Into what part of the Basilisk did Harry plunge the sword?

265. What colour robes does Hufflepuff house play Quidditch in?

266. What was the first name of the Hogwarts founder, Gryffindor?

267. On Harry's last evening with the Weasleys, what entertainment did Fred and George provide?

268. What item did Harry try on again in Dumbledore's office?

269. Which Professor announces to the school that the Mandrake plants are matured: Sprout, McGonagall or Snape?

270. How did people who had read *Sonnets of a Sorcerer* speak for the rest of their lives?

271. What spell, beginning with the letter L, causes the end of a wand to light up?

272. Who was, unusually, staying at Hogwarts for Christmas?

273. Through what device's reflection had Hermione seen the Basilisk?

274. How many Valentines Day cards did Lockhart claim he had received?

275. What creature is born from a chicken's egg and hatched underneath a toad?

276. What spell does Malfoy use to conjure up a snake to attack Harry in Duelling Club?

277. Who was the only person believed to be able to open the Chamber of Secrets?

278. What happens to the envelope of a Howler after it has been delivered?

279. Who, in Herbology class, apologises to Harry for thinking he was Slytherin's heir?

280. Whose nose swelled to the size of a melon during Professor Snape's potions class?

281. Who is the subject of the giant statue in the Chamber of Secrets?

282. From whose stores were Hermione, Harry and Ron going to steal some Boomslang skin?

283. In what lesson do Harry and Ron spot spiders heading towards the Forbidden Forest?

284. How many points does a team receive for catching the Golden Snitch?

285. Who catches Ron and Harry in the first floor girls' toilets?

286. How long did Professor Binns ask for homework on the Medieval Assembly of European Wizards to be?

287. On whose table did Harry leave his Invisibility Cloak before heading into the Forbidden Forest?

288. What is the name of the language used to speak to snakes?

289. Who is Ron's duelling partner in second-year Duelling Club?

290. In which Dark Arts shop does Harry arrive after using Floo powder for the first time?

291. What book do Harry, Hermione and Ron obtain from the Restricted Section of the library?

292. What words does Riddle rearrange 'Tom Marvolo Riddle' into?

293. What was Tom Riddle's father's first name?

294. Who was captain of the Slytherin Quidditch team?

295. What colour does Ron's bedroom appear to Harry?

296. What does Professor Dumbledore decide has happened to Mrs Norris?

297. Which professor wasn't sitting at the high table during the sorting ceremony?

298. What game did the headless horsemen start to play during Nick's speech?

299. Whose parents were changing Muggle money into wizard money at Gringotts?

300. What creature is Mrs Mason very afraid of?

Questions about Harry Potter and the Prisoner of Azkaban

1. What does Professor Lupin turn into?

2. What village are third-year students at Hogwarts sometimes allowed to visit?

3. Which poltergeist woke Harry up early on the morning of the first Quidditch match of the season?

4. Which lesson did Hermione storm out of: Divination, Transfiguration or Arithmancy?

5. What is the name of the building supposed to be the most haunted in Britain?

6. What magazine carries reviews and tests of different broomsticks?

7. Who is Head Boy of Hogwarts in Harry's third year?

8. How many years did Sirius Black spend in Azkaban before escaping: six, ten or twelve?

9. Which exam was held at midnight?

10. Which painting was found slashed, and its subject vanished, in October at Hogwarts?

11. What is the name of the small hour-glass on a gold chain, which Hermione uses to go back in time?

12. A portrait of a fat lady in a pink dress guarded the entrance to which Hogwarts house?

13. Against which house do Gryffindor play their first Quidditch match of the season?

14. Who has a sister Harry has to refer to as Aunt Marge?

15. Is Marcus Flint, Cedric Diggory or Oliver Wood captain of Hufflepuff's Quidditch team?

16. What was Harry's favourite Christmas present?

17. What is the name of the vehicle that provides emergency transport for stranded witches and wizards?

18. Who won the Quidditch match between Ravenclaw and Slytherin?

19. Harry received birthday presents from Ron, Hermione and which other friend from Hogwarts?

20. What sort of items does the shop called Honeydukes sell?

21. What happened to Professor Lupin when the clouds moved to show a full moon?

22. Which female teacher had first suggested Harry should join his house Quidditch team?

23. Hermione, Ron and Harry passed all their exams: true or false?

24. Who had given Harry a tough summer holiday essay about Shrinking Potions?

25. Who is Harry's godfather?

26. Which pub does Madam Rosmerta serve at: the Leaky Cauldron, the Three Broomsticks or the Wizard and Wand?

27. The witch at the Magical Menagerie suggests Rat Tonic will revive which pet?

28. Where does Cornelius Fudge suggest Harry takes a room for the last two weeks of the holiday?

29. Who gives Harry some anti-Dementor lessons?

30. Which house won the Quidditch Cup?

31. What three birds entered Harry's room through the window the night of his thirteenth birthday?

32. Who confiscated Harry's new Firebolt broomstick as a security measure?

33. Which Professor do Harry, Ron and Hermione spot on the Hogwarts Express?

34. Is Professor Flitwick's office on the third, fifth or seventh floor?

35. Who did Neville Longbottom fear the most in all the world?

36. What sporting event is on in the summer between Harry's third and fourth year?

37. What colour was the Knight Bus which rescued Harry?

38. What prison fortess lies on a small island out at sea?

39. In the middle of which lesson does Draco Malfoy return from the hospital wing?

40. Who did Ron think slashed the curtains in the Gryffindor third-year dormitory?

41. At what building in Hogsmeade did Harry and Ron see over 300 owls?

42. What subject does Professor Lupin teach?

43. Hermione uses an Alohomora spell to: open a window, shrink Draco Malfoy or put Ron to sleep?

44. Who does Scabbers the rat turn out to be?

45. Is Buckbeak's appeal the day Harry and his friends start, or finish, their exams?

46. Do Kappas live in the air, in water or on land?

47. How many decks did the Knight Bus have: one, two or three?

48. Who escaped the executioner and the Dementors on the back of a hippogriff?

49. Did Aunt Marge shrink to the size of a pin, grow as high as the house or swell so that she was completely round?

50. What creature did Seamus Finnigan turn the Boggart into: a banshee, a mummy or a severed hand?

51. What is the only non-Muggle settlement in the whole of Britain?

52. What tree destroyed Harry's Quidditch broomstick?

53. What was the name of the person who escaped from Azkaban?

54. What creature beginning with the letter B likes enclosed spaces and is a shape-shifter?

55. Where would you find the store called Dervish and Banges?

56. Which professor found Harry, Ron, Hermione and Sirius Black?

57. What new item of wizarding equipment does Ron show Harry within minutes of meeting him in the summer?

58. Who says that Harry's father would have saved Pettigrew, just like Harry did?

59. As what animal did Sirius Black escape from Azkaban?

60. Who sends Ron a tiny owl to replace his pet rat?

61. Harry goes with Ron and Hermione for their first visit to Hogsmeade: true or false?

62. Which European country did Hermione and her family visit for their summer holidays?

63. What injury did Ron suffer from being dragged away by the giant black dog?

64. The Marauder's Map shows the movements of people around Hogwarts: true or false?

65. Who admits to betraying Harry's parents to Lord Voldemort?

66. A hundred or so of what creatures caused Harry to hear a screaming woman and fall off his broom?

67. Who was in Harry's room at the Leaky Cauldron as Harry first opened the door?

68. Who received a Howler letter from his grandmother?

69. Who calls a telephone a fellytone by mistake?

70. What sort of creature does Hermione buy from the Magical Menagerie as a pet?

71. A pet cat trying to capture and eat a pet rat saw which two Hogwarts students fall out?

72. Outside which building did the Knight Bus drop Harry?

73. What was Ron, Harry and Hermione's last exam: Divination, Astronomy or Ancient Runes?

74. Professor Lupin is always ill at full moon: true or false?

75. Fleetwood's High-Finish Handle Polish is used on what wizarding item?

76. Where did Harry, Hermione and Ron have a drink of delicious Butterbeer?

77. What new school subject for Harry begins with the letter D?

78. Is Cho Chang a third-year, fourth-year or fifth-year at Hogwarts?

79. Is the landlord of the Leaky Cauldron called Tom, Tim or Jim?

80. Is a Grindylow a type of hippogriff, water demon, banshee or Red Cap?

81. Who won the House Championship for the third year running?

82. Where does Harry ask the Knight Bus to take him?

83. Who refused to let Sirius Black into Gryffindor Tower?

84. The Weasley family went to China for their summer holidays: true or false?

85. Who won the Ravenclaw v Gryffindor Quidditch match?

86. What is the name of the new broomstick believed to be the fastest in the world?

87. Who stops Lupin and Black from killing Peter Pettigrew?

88. Percy Weasley failed his N.E.W.T. exams: true or false?

89. What did passengers on the Knight Bus rest on?

90. What is a new school subject for Harry's third year: Potions, Care of Magical Creatures or Defence Against the Dark Arts?

91. What colour fur does Hermione's pet cat have?

92. Apart from James Potter, name one of Professor Lupin's other two friends when he was a Hogwarts student?

93. Who grabbed hold of Harry's broom just as he was gaining on the Golden Snitch?

94. Who performs a spell to make Harry's glasses repel water?

95. Who have the Dursleys said is attending St Brutus's Secure Centre for Incurably Criminal Boys?

96. Whose father does Lupin say transformed himself into a stag?

97. Who offers Harry a home away from the Dursleys?

98. Harry's summer holiday homework involved writing about: William the Wise, Wendelin the Weird or Frederick the Fanciful?

99. Around whose arm does the giant black dog fix his teeth?

100. Where would you find the Three Broomsticks pub?

101. What can a wizard who is an Animagus do?

102. What movement should you make when approaching a Hippogriff: a wave, a bow or fall to your knees?

103. Which job does Macnair perform: Knight Bus driver, Boggart hunter or executioner?

104. Who is the captain of the Gryffindor Quidditch team?

105. Who resigns from his teaching position at Hogwarts after Sirius Black escapes?

106. What is Madam Pomfrey's first name: Poppy, Lupin, Rose or Ivy?

107. Who slapped Malfoy around the face after he had mocked Hagrid crying?

108. What is the name of the wizarding game similar to marbles?

109. What device does Hermione use secretly all year to take her many lessons?

110. Which Hogwarts student used a telephone for the first time in trying to contact Harry?

111. What sort of creature, beginning with the letter G, did Professor Lupin show Harry while the others were away?

112. What was to take place on the first Saturday after the Easter Holidays?

113. Which member of the Weasley family works as a curse breaker in Egypt?

114. What creature is used instead of a Dementor for Harry's anti-Dementor lessons?

115. What creature boarded the Hogwarts Express and caused Harry to feel ill?

116. Sirius Black is an Animagus: true or false?

117. Who does Cornelius Fudge say betrayed Harry's parents to Lord Voldemort?

118. Buckbeak, a Hippogriff, injures which student in Harry's first Care of Magical Creatures lesson?

119. Whose nickname as a Hogwarts student was Prongs?

120. What did the Weasleys spend their prize winnings on over the summer?

121. Who wrote all of the week's passwords for Gryffindor down on a piece of paper?

122. What was the only item needed for Professor Lupin's first lesson?

123. Which teacher at Hogwarts has Remus as their first name?

124. Whose spell knocks Professor Snape out in front of Sirius Black and Professor Lupin?

125. Who plays Seeker for Ravenclaw in Harry's third year?

126. In what country does the Knight Bus drop off a passenger before Harry?

127. Which Professor catches Harry with Neville at the entrance to the secret passage to Hogsmeade?

128. What creature has the body of a horse but the head and wings of an eagle?

129. Whose arm injury prevented Slytherin from playing a Quidditch game when they should have?

130. Who whacked Harry around the shins to stop him winning musical statues at Dudley's fifth birthday party?

131. Who uses Ron's wand to remove Harry and Hermione's wands from their hands?

132. What is the name of the dog Aunt Marge brings with her to the Dursleys?

133. The Whomping Willow was planted the year which professor first arrived at Hogwarts: Professor Lupin, Professor Snape or Professor Flitwick?

134. What device led Lupin to find Harry, his friends and Sirius Black?

135. What did Florean Fortescue give Harry for free every half an hour?

136. In what shop in Hogsmeade did Harry appear and surprise Ron and Hermione?

137. Who whisked Harry away from Professor Snape after he was caught sneaking back from Hogsmeade?

138. What item does not come in a Broomstick Servicing Kit: a compass, a broom cloth or a pair of tail twig clippers?

139. What part of the body is Scabbers the rat missing?

140. Who calls Harry and Hermione into her office the moment they arrive at Hogwarts?

141. Which creature do Harry and Hermione save from execution?

142. How long did Hagrid spend in Azkaban in Harry's second year: two weeks, one month or two months?

143. Who replaces the Fat Lady as guardian of Gryffindor Tower?

144. Who does Sirius Black say was the Secret-Keeper for Harry's parents: Lupin, Snape, Peter Pettigrew or Dumbledore?

145. What subject did Professor Trelawney teach Harry at Hogwarts?

146. What creatures are to be banished from the Hogwarts grounds after attempting to kill Harry?

147. Florean Fortescue ran a bookshop, an ice-cream parlour or a cauldron shop in Diagon Alley?

148. What is the name of the goblin-like creatures that haunt battlefields, dungeons and other places where blood has been shed?

149. The Hogwarts Express is usually used by students and not teachers: true or false?

150. Which subject's exam involved an obstacle course containing Hinkypunks and Red Caps?

151. Whose teacup in Divination class bears the sign of the Grim, the omen of death?

152. Four members of which Hogwarts house dressed up as Dementors to scare Harry?

153. How high off the ground were the hoops in Quidditch: 50 feet, 100 feet or 150 feet?

154. Who caused Harry to blush when she wished him good luck just before the match against Slytherin?

155. What was the name of the cat that tried to attack Scabbers in the Magical Menagerie?

156. Who was the best friend of Sirius Black when they were students at Hogwarts?

157. What present did Harry receive from Hermione for his birthday?

158. Who did Peter Pettigrew try to corner only to be blown to pieces?

159. What happened to the player who lost a point in a game of Gobstones?

160. A bunch of security trolls were hired to guard what feature at the entrance of Gryffindor Tower?

161. How many Dementors did Harry see during the final Quidditch match of the season?

162. Was it on the first, third or last day of Aunt Marge's visit that Harry escaped the Dursleys?

163. How many students apart from Ron, Hermione and Harry were at Hogwarts for Christmas: none, one, three or five?

164. People wearing invisibility cloaks do not show up on the Marauder's Map: true or false?

165. Who replaced Professor Kettleburn for Care of Magical Creatures lessons?

166. Who does Hermione think sent Harry the Firebolt broomstick?

167. Cassandra Vablatsky was the author of what 'foggy'-titled book?

168. What creature leaps on Harry when he and Hermione are under the Invisibility Cloak?

169. A Patronus is: a shield between a person and a Dementor, an old model of broomstick or a junior official at the Ministry of Magic?

170. What colour were the cars from the Ministry of Magic, which ferried the Weasleys to King's Cross station?

171. Who had a bet on with Penelope Clearwater over the outcome of the Ravenclaw v Gryffindor Quidditch match?

172. Who suggested Hermione and Harry go back in time to save Sirius Black?

173. What food did Professor Lupin give Harry after his first encounter with a Dementor?

174. What was the easiest of all of Harry and Ron's exams?

175. Is Hermione taking all of these new subjects: Divination, Muggle Studies, Study of Ancient Runes and Arithmancy?

176. Which student did Professor Lupin prevent from taking on the Boggart in the wardrobe?

177. Did Harry buy *Intermediate Transfiguration, Advanced Divination* or *Spells for Beginners* from Flourish and Blotts?

178. What creatures surrounded Harry, Hermione and Sirius Black?

179. Which teacher was incredibly thin and wore a shawl and lots of bangles?

180. What creature can clamp its jaws around a person's mouth and suck out their soul?

181. Which of the following was not a maker of the Marauder's Map: Padfoot, Prongs, Wormhead, Moony?

182. Outside what sort of store did Harry meet Ron and Hermione in the summer holidays?

183. Which member of the Weasley family was sitting exams tougher than Ordinary Wizarding Levels?

184. What is the name of the device that lights up and spins when someone untrustworthy is around?

185. Professor Lupin performs a *Ferula* spell to bandage and splint whose leg?

186. Who has a new wand for the third year made of willow and containing a single unicorn tail-hair?

187. Which one of Harry's friends had to write an essay called 'Explain why Muggles Need Electricity'?

188. How many Animagi were listed in the official records of the 20th century: one, seven, eleven or 24?

189. What did Fred and George Weasley change Percy's Head Boy badge to read?

190. Harry left his wand in the changing rooms before his Quidditch match with Ravenclaw: true or false?

191. The first term of Divination lessons were to be devoted to reading what?

192. What cat communicated with Sirius Black and stole the passwords to Gryffindor tower for him?

193. What job does Stan Shunpike perform?

194. How many accurate predictions does Dumbledore say that Professor Trelawney has made: one, two or seven?

195. Which member of the Dursley family hates animals?

196. What creature was involved in the Care of Magical Creatures exam?

197. Who bought Harry a copy of the *Monster Book of Monsters*?

198. Who magicked Harry onto a stretcher after he'd fallen from his broom?

199. What sort of creature does Aunt Marge breed at her house in the country?

200. What sort of food did Professor Lupin give Harry after each attempt at the Patronus spell?

201. What mark did Hermione get in her Muggle Studies exam: 99%, 100%, 200% or 320%?

202. Which teacher at Hogwarts was one of the four makers of the Marauder's Map?

203. Who was Best Man at the wedding of Harry's parents?

204. What are Professor Lupin's initials?

205. What is the name of the spell that forces a Boggart into a shape people find funny?

206. Who liked being burned as a witch so much that she allowed herself to be caught 47 times?

207. What other exam clashes with Hermione's Ancient Runes exam?

208. How many secret passages lead from Hogwarts to Hogsmeade?

209. Professor Snape insists that Neville Longbottom tries out his Shrinking Solution on what creature?

210. What creature does Ron place the tiny owl near, to check that it is real?

211. In which month is Hermione's birthday?

212. Who is summoned to attend a hearing of the Committee for the Disposal of Dangerous Creatures in April?

213. What is the name of the potion made by Professor Snape and drunk every month by Professor Lupin?

214. What present did Ron buy Harry for his birthday?

215. What did Percy hope to do if he passed his tough exams?

216. Who caught the Golden Snitch in the first Quidditch match of the season?

217. What did Harry use to keep the *Monster Book of Monsters* shut?

218. Who hugs Harry when he arrives back at King's Cross, after his third year at Hogwarts?

219. What magical creature does Hagrid show the class in his first lesson?

220. Who was the last Gryffindor Seeker to help win the Quidditch Cup?

221. Filch the caretaker knows about how many of the secret passageways from Hogwarts to Hogsmeade: two, four, five or six?

222. Which student attacked the Boggart in the wardrobe first?

223. What happened when the two Slytherin Beaters tried to hit Harry?

224. How do you open the *Monster Book of Monsters* safely?

225. Who wrote down permission for Harry to visit Hogsmeade in his fourth year?

226. What was the name of the unconscious owl carried by two other owls into Harry's bedroom?

227. How many hours back in time do Harry and Hermione go to save Sirius Black?

228. Which subject did Professor Kettleburn teach at Hogwarts before retiring?

229. Who, along with Malfoy, Goyle and Crabbe, dressed up as Dementors?

230. Who do Ron, Harry and Hermione believe influenced the decision to execute Buckbeak?

231. Who was given a detention for criticising Professor Snape's teaching methods?

232. At what time of year does Professor Trelawney predict that one of their number will leave for ever?

233. Into what building did Harry, Hermione and Buckbeak head to avoid being discovered?

234. How many Galleons formed the first prize in the *Daily Prophet* Prize Galleon Draw?

235. Who does Cornelius Fudge say will get an Order of Merlin Second Class?

236. According to Mr Weasley, how many times had Harry and Ron ended up in the Forbidden Forest before starting their third year?

237. What device did Professor Lupin use to know Harry was about to visit him before he left?

238. What stuffed creature topped the witch's hat that came out of the cracker Dumbledore and Snape pulled?

239. What was the name of the driver of the Knight Bus?

240. For how many years have Gryffindor not won the Quidditch Cup?

241. Were Sirius Black and James Potter in their first, third, fifth or sixth years when they managed to turn into animals?

242. Was Ron's new wand nine inches, eleven inches or fourteen inches long?

243. Which subject does Hermione decide to drop for her fourth year?

244. Where does Harry hide his homework and birthday cards in the Dursleys' house?

245. How many years did the woman at the Magical Menagerie say was the normal lifespan of a rat?

246. Which Professor goes into a trance and states that Lord Voldemort's servant will join him before midnight?

247. What department was sent to the Dursleys' to deflate Aunt Marge?

248. Who told Professor Dumbledore that Sirius Black had arrived?

249. What hit Harry and Hermione moments after the giant black dog attacked?

250. Who won the annual *Daily Prophet* Grand Prize Galleon Draw?

251. Who conjured up stretchers to carry Harry, Ron, Hermione and Sirius Black back to Hogwarts?

252. Madam Hooch and which Professor were going to strip Harry's new broomstick to check it was free of jinxes?

253. What is the first name of Draco Malfoy's crony, Crabbe?

254. Who surprised Lupin, Black, Harry and his friends by entering the room using Harry's Invisibility Cloak?

255. How many seconds does it take a Firebolt to accelerate from 0 to 150 mph?

256. Who lent Sirius Black a newspaper while he was in Azkaban?

257. How many weeks of the summer holiday did Harry go without contact from his school friends?

258. What creatures looked like scaly monkeys and strangled people in ponds?

259. What creature did Harry conjure up to repel the Dementors: a stag, a unicorn or a Boggart?

260. Where were all the students of Hogwarts told to sleep on Hallowe'en night?

261. Which knight in a painting helped Harry, Ron and Hermione find their Divination lesson?

262. What false name does Harry first use to the conductor of the Knight Bus?

263. What was Sirius Black's nickname as a Hogwarts student: Prongs, Wormtail or Padfoot?

264. Who wrote *A History of Magic*?

265. What number is Sirius Black's vault at Gringott's Bank: 911, 711 or 811?

266. For how many people was the Christmas dinner table set in the Great Hall?

267. What was the largest part of Peter Pettigrew's body that was recovered?

268. What was the number of the room that Harry took at the Leaky Cauldron?

269. Which two words does one say to wipe the Marauder's Map clean?

270. Who did Harry see on the other side of the lake, ward off the Dementors?

271. Who did Harry bump into the second he left the Knight Bus?

272. Which two people chained themselves to Peter Pettigrew?

273. How many dogs does Aunt Marge have in total?

274. What did students have to turn a teapot into during their Transfiguration exam?

275. Whose rabbit, Binky, was killed by a fox?

276. The Knight Bus fare to London is eleven Sickles, but what does one get if one pays thirteen Sickles?

277. Which Professor surprisingly joined the others for Christmas dinner?

278. Who does Professor Trelawney predict will be late for their second Divination lesson?

279. To which room does Professor Lupin take his class to expel a Boggart?

280. Who gave Harry the Marauder's Map?

281. Who tells a teacher that Harry received a broomstick for Christmas with no note or card?

282. Which student offered to forge the signature on Harry's Hogsmeade permission form?

283. Who was the only girl in the Ravenclaw Quidditch team?

284. What was the name of the road in which Harry first saw the Knight Bus?

285. By how many points did Gryffindor lose their first Quidditch match of the season?

286. Which Gryffindor player saves Slytherin's penalty?

287. How many Christmas trees decorated the Great Hall at Hogwarts?

288. What present did Aunt Marge give Harry the year she bought Dudley a computerised robot?

289. Which important wizarding adult did Harry meet straight after his last-but-one exam?

290. How many house points did Ron lose Gryffindor when he threw a crocodile heart at Malfoy?

291. What item, apart from the Marauder's Map, does Lupin hand to Harry before leaving?

292. How many house points does Professor Snape take from Gryffindor for Hermione helping Neville with his Shrinking Solution?

293. What is the name of the small, one-legged creature that lures people into bogs?

294. How many people was Sirius Black supposed to have killed with a single curse?

295. Who gave Hermione a Time-Turner on the first day of the school year at Hogwarts?

296. Where does Harry send his owl, Hedwig, when Aunt Marge visits?

297. What creature does Professor Snape insist they learn about when he takes over Professor Lupin's class?

298. What spell, beginning with the letter N, switches off the light at the end of a wand?

299. Whose nostril became filled with chewing gum after Professor Lupin performed a *Waddiwasi* spell?

300. What electrical device did the Dursleys buy for Dudley's welcome-home-for-the-summer present?

Questions about Harry Potter and the Goblet of Fire

1. How many schools take part in the Triwizard Tournament?

2. Who surprises Harry by partnering Viktor Krum at the Yule Ball?

3. Rita Skeeter is a reporter on which wizarding newspaper?

4. Who does Ron finally ask for an autograph just as everyone leaves Hogwarts?

5. Which member of the Dursley family was on a diet during the summer holidays?

6. What bird is found on the Hogwarts coat of arms?

7. Which ghost startles Harry as he takes a bath in the Prefects' Bathroom?

8. Did the delegation from Durmstrang arrive by air, land or water?

9. What is the name of the rival wizarding school beginning with the letter B?

10. Who has a tiny pet owl called Pig?

11. Which of Hagrid's parents was a giant?

12. For which country did the Seeker, Aidan Lynch, play Quidditch?

13. Blast-Ended Skrewts are the subject of whose first lesson?

14. Who was champion of Durmstrang school?

15. In what golden item is a puzzle contained for the second Triwizard task?

16. What happens to leprechaun gold after a few hours?

17. What is the name of the house-elf that Harry and the others sit next to at the Quidditch World Cup?

18. Who hopes to return to England to improve her English?

19. What sort of creatures did Harry have to go and seek in the lake at Hogwarts?

20. What colour is the Slytherin banner?

21. What was the surname of the father and son that Harry, Hermione and the Weasleys met at Stoatshead Hill?

22. Which professor repeatedly predicted Harry's death?

23. Which musical group played at the Yule Ball?

24. How long was the gigantic snake that Frank Bryce saw: eight feet, twelve feet or 20 feet long?

25. Who tied Harry to a gravestone on Lord Voldemort's orders?

26. Is the lion on the Gryffindor banner silver, bronze or gold?

27. What sort of shop do Fred and George Weasley hope to open?

28. What object was used to select the champions for the Triwizard Tournament?

29. With which creatures does Dumbledore tell Fudge that the Ministry should make an alliance: giants, Death Eaters or Dementors?

30. Who sent Harry some pasties and a huge fruit cake for the summer holidays?

31. What item did Dobby wear on his head as a hat?

32. How many tables are there in the Great Hall: three, four, five or six?

33. Professor Grubbly-Plank takes over from which Hogwarts teacher?

34. Approximately how many wizards were expected to turn up to watch the Quidditch World Cup?

35. Which organiser of the Quidditch World Cup was in debt to Goblins?

36. Who, at number four Privet Drive, throws china ornaments at Mr Weasley?

37. Malfoy's *Densaugeo* spell hit Hermione, causing what part of her to grow?

38. Who does Hagrid believe is a half-giant like himself?

39. Professor Sprout was the Death Eater at Hogwarts still loyal to Voldemort: true or false?

40. Viktor Krum invited Hermione to Bulgaria for the summer: true or false?

41. Which Hogwarts student famously survived an *Avada Kedavra* curse?

42. Which member of the Weasley family has a ponytail and an earring?

43. What sweet invention of Fred and George Weasley turned Neville into a bird for a few moments?

44. For which team did Ludo Bagman play Quidditch: the Chudley Cannons, the Wimbourne Wasps or the Woodlands Wanderers?

45. No non-human creature is permitted to carry a wand: true or false?

46. What giant creature does Harry save Cedric from in view of the Triwizard Cup?

47. Who has a wooden leg with its end carved into a clawed foot?

48. What is Professor Karkaroff's first name: Ivan, Igor, Gregor or Albus?

49. What object did Harry use to help him succeed in the first Triwizard Tournament task?

50. How old was Harry when Lord Voldemort killed his parents?

51. How many Unforgiveable Curses are there?

52. In which month does the second Triwizard Tournament task take place?

53. Who has a sign in the sky known as the Dark Mark?

54. What is the surname of Percy Weasley's boss?

55. The destroyer of dangerous beasts, Macnair, is a Death Eater: true or false?

56. Which newspaper reporter interviews Harry at the Wand Weighing ceremony?

57. Harry writes to someone, who the Dursleys are terrified will turn up at their house; who is it?

58. Who did Harry give his thousand Galleons prize to?

59. Flying carpets were banned by wizards in Britain: true or false?

60. What is the surname of the retired wizard known as Mad-Eye?

61. What colour does Dudley's tongue turn when it grows over a foot long?

62. In what month did the delegations from Beauxbatons and Durmstrang arrive at Hogwarts?

63. Which Hogwarts student was the first to form a group to protect house-elves?

64. Who asks to speak to Harry alone after the briefing for the third Triwizard task?

65. Which country plays Ireland in the Quidditch World Cup final?

66. What end of year event did Triwizard champions not have to take part in?

67. Who is Hogwarts' new Defence Against the Dark Arts teacher?

68. Which student does Rita Skeeter say is Harry's girlfriend?

69. What viewing device allows you to replay action and slow down what you are watching?

70. With whom does Hagrid hope to perform a job over the summer for Dumbledore?

71. Where would you find the largest group of house-elves in Britain?

72. What object is used to transport wizards from one place to another at an arranged time?

73. Did Harry go first, second or last in the first Triwizard task?

74. Who was killed by an *Avada Kedavra* curse whilst standing next to Harry?

75. What colour is the Gryffindor banner: red, orange or purple?

76. Which country won the Quidditch World Cup final?

77. How tall was the hedge that was part of the third Triwizard task: ten feet, 20 feet, 30 feet or 40 feet high?

78. What name did supporters of Lord Voldemort give themselves: Dark Siders, Death Eaters or Dementors?

79. Who was Harry supposed to rescue from the lake for his second Triwizard task?

80. Who, in a temper, threw a badge that hit Ron Weasley on the forehead?

81. Which wizarding school is believed to be in the far north because the students wear fur capes?

82. Harry issues an *Expelliarmus* spell as who tries to attack him with an *Avada Kedavra* curse?

83. What creature did Professor Grubbly-Plank bring to her first lesson?

84. The Department of Magical Transportation fines people for Apparating without a licence: true or false?

85. How many years had passed since the Dark Mark had been seen: thirteen, 50 or 100 years?

86. Who gives Harry some Gillyweed before the second Triwizard task?

87. Who is the only person not to believe that Lord Voldemort has returned?

88. How much does Mr Weasley bet on the Quidditch World Cup match: one Sickle, one Galleon or five Galleons?

89. What colour is the Dark Mark skull in the sky: light blue, emerald green or blood red?

90. What colour are unicorn foals?

91. Out of which material was the Goblet of Fire made: wood, glass or gold?

92. What country's Quidditch team has a player called Viktor Krum?

93. How many Galleons does the winner of the Triwizard Tournament receive?

94. Who did Harry first ask to be his partner at the Yule Ball?

95. Whose name was the fourth to come out of the Goblet of Fire?

96. Who writes a letter to the Dursleys with the envelope almost completely covered in stamps?

97. In what month did the third task in the Triwizard Tournament take place?

98. Who caught the Golden Snitch in the Quidditch World Cup final?

99. Who caught Rita Skeeter and placed her in a glass jar?

100. In which month did Harry's two best friends send him birthday cards?

101. Which house banner features a black badger?

102. What word means to disappear from one place and reappear almost straight away in another?

103. Parvati Patel goes to the Yule Ball with whom?

104. Who shows Dumbledore and the others in the hospital wing the sign of the Dark Mark on his arm?

105. How old is Rita Skeeter: 34, 37, 43 or 109?

106. At what age do Hogwarts students take Ordinary Wizarding Levels?

107. Who does Professor Moody turn into a white ferret?

108. What did Viktor Krum try to transfigure into to complete the second Triwizard task?

109. What social event is a traditional part of the Triwizard Tournament?

110. How long does Lord Voldemort tell Wormtail they will be staying in the Riddle House?

111. Viktor Krum was under an Imperius curse when he attacked Cedric Diggory in the maze: true or false?

112. What mark out of ten did Ludo Bagman award Harry for his first Triwizard task?

113. How long is Professor Moody going to be Defence Against the Dark Arts teacher?

114. Who did Cedric Diggory have to free from the lake in the Triwizard tournament?

115. On what day of the week does the final of the Quidditch World Cup occur?

116. When the Triwizard families meet, who is there for Harry?

117. Who told Professor Moody that Neville Longbottom was very good at Herbology?

118. What creatures had greyish skins and long, dark green hair?

119. A wand works even better than usual when it meets its brother: true or false?

120. How tall are giants usually: ten feet, twelve feet, 20 feet or 30 feet?

121. Which professor can see through Harry's Invisibility Cloak?

122. What sort of creatures delivered Sirius Black's letters to Harry at Privet Drive?

123. Who went first in the first task of the Triwizard Tournament?

124. Who does Ron rudely call 'Vicky'?

125. How many birthday cards did Harry receive in total?

126. Which former England Quidditch player was put on trial for passing information to Lord Voldemort's supporters?

127. Who sent his own son to Azkaban?

128. What colour is the Ravenclaw banner?

129. Bertha Jorkins was killed by whom?

130. What happens if you don't open a Howler letter immediately?

131. Who does Hermione make treasurer of S.P.E.W.?

132. Which of the following weren't dragons used in the Triwizard Tournament: Chinese Fireball, Latvian Long-Snout, Common Welsh Green?

133. Did Troy, Krum, Ivanova or Moran make the first score of the Quidditch World Cup final?

134. What is the first name of Colin Creevey's brother?

135. Who repairs Henry's injured leg with tears: Fawkes, Dumbledore, Sirius Black or Madam Pomfrey?

136. On which day of the week did Harry have his first lesson with Professor Moody?

137. Who saved Gabrielle Delacour from the lake?

138. Who bought Harry a knife with attachments to unlock locks and untie knots?

139. Would you find an otter, a badger, a cat or a hedgehog on the Hogwarts coat of arms?

140. Wales were beaten at the Quidditch World Cup by Uganda, Rwanda or Algeria?

141. Who casts a spell to replace Wormtail's missing hand?

142. Who was head of Hufflepuff house?

143. What is the name of the fluffy black creature which likes seeking out treasure?

144. Which Hogwarts student's mother is called Narcissa?

145. Two crossed golden wands are on the coat of arms of which school?

146. The Weird Sisters are a female Quidditch team, a musical group or a squad of banshees?

147. Both Goyle's and Crabbe's fathers are Death Eaters: true or false?

148. What creature did the fake wand Fred and George showed Ludo Bagman turn into?

149. What was the gruesome name of the pub in Little Hangleton?

150. Which ghost does Harry meet whilst underwater in the lake?

151. How old was Viktor Krum at the Quidditch World Cup?

152. Which Death Eater is the father of one of Harry's least favourite Hogwarts students?

153. Was Mr Jones, Mr Roberts, Mr Payne or Mr Reynolds the manager of the campsite where Harry and the Weasleys stayed?

154. Which professor do Harry and Ron see talking to Karkaroff when they walk away from the Yule Ball?

155. On what creature does Professor Moody demonstrate the Imperius curse?

156. Which Professor rudely says he sees no change to Hermione after she is hit by Malfoy's spell?

157. Who put a compensation claim in for a destroyed twelve-bedroomed tent with jacuzzi: Barty Crouch, Viktor Krum or Mundungus Fletcher?

158. How long was the Blast-Ended Skrewt Harry encountered in the maze: three feet, seven feet, ten feet or fourteen feet long?

159. Which Quidditch team hat did Ron receive as a Christmas present?

160. Lavender Brown and Parvati Patil admire which teacher?

161. What was the name of Fred and George Weasley's tongue-growing sweets?

162. Who received hate mail which put boils on her hands?

163. What minimum age does Professor Dumbledore say competitors for the Triwizard Tournament have to be?

164. Who is the head of the Department of Magical Games and Sports?

165. Who became Hogwarts gamekeeper after he was expelled from the school as a student?

166. Who caught Karkaroff and got him sent to the prison at Azkaban?

167. Was the Triwizard Tournament started over 400, over 700 or over 900 years ago?

168. Blast-Ended Skrewts hibernate in winter: true or false?

169. Cuthbert Mockridge is head of the Department for Magical Charms, the Goblin Liaison Office or the Dragon Handling Committee?

170. Which language do Goblins often speak: Veela, Bulgarian, Banshee or Gobbledygook?

171. What is the name of the owl that brings a letter from Sirius Black to Harry at Hogwarts?

172. What name does Sirius Black ask Ron, Harry and Hermione to use when talking about him?

173. What present did Dobby buy Harry for Christmas?

174. What is the name, starting with the letter A, given to people who were Dark-wizard-catchers?

175. What item in the maze turns out to be a Portkey?

176. What position did Ludo Bagman play at Quidditch?

177. Which wizarding school's robes were a blood red colour?

178. Who drops water bombs on the students as they arrive at Hogwarts?

179. Who named the owl, Pidwidgeon, which Ron calls Pig for short?

180. Who drew an Age Line around the Goblet of Fire?

181. Who did Harry intend sharing the Triwizard Cup with?

182. What event does Professor Dumbledore announce will not take place this year?

183. Which Beauxbatons student snubbed Ron's invitation to attend the Yule Ball as his partner?

184. Which first-year fell in the lake on the way to Hogwarts?

185. What was the name of the creature that the Bulgarians brought as Quidditch mascots?

186. Who does Ron believe that Hagrid has a crush on?

187. Who advises Harry to take the golden egg into a bath?

188. Who causes the glass window of the train carriage door to shatter by slamming it in a temper?

189. What colour was the Beauxbatons carriage?

190. Is 'cobbing' a Quidditch foul, a way of taming dragons or a method of growing magical plants?

191. Who helped Harry back to Hogwarts castle after his battle with Lord Voldemort?

192. Fanged Frisbees and Screaming Yo-yos can be used in Hogwarts only by fourth- and fifth-years: true or false?

193. What was the nationality of the wizard who refereed the final of the Quidditch World Cup?

194. Who checks the wands of those entering the Triwizard Tournament?

195. Who gives Harry the prize money for winning the Triwizard Tournament?

196. How many pairs of Omnioculars did Harry buy?

197. What colour were Ron's new dress robes with lace cuffs?

198. Who manages to throw off Professor Moody's Imperius curse in a lesson?

199. In what European country did Lord Voldemort capture Bertha Jorkins: Albania, Slovenia or Bulgaria?

200. Which entrant to the Triwizard Tournament is part Veela?

201. Who was the first ghost to come out of the end of Lord Voldemort's wand?

202. What word, beginning with the letter S, means to leave half of yourself behind when Apparating?

203. What does WWN stand for?

204. How many people have survived an *Avada Kedavra* curse?

205. What does the potion Veritaserum make the taker do?

206. What sort of potion do Fred and George Weasley use to try to put their names into the Goblet of Fire?

207. In which village would you find the Riddle House?

208. What hits Viktor Krum in the nose during the Quidditch World Cup final?

209. Who refereed the final of the Quidditch World Cup?

210. What was the name on the gravestone Harry was tied to?

211. What is the password to open the Prefects' bathroom?

212. How many mammals are found on the Hogwarts coat of arms?

213. Which two house-elves without owners did Professor Dumbledore give jobs at Hogwarts?

214. Snape starts reading an article about Harry out of which wizarding publication?

215. How many items are there on Mr Filch's list of forbidden objects at Hogwarts: 159, 342, 437 or 982?

216. In the form of what creature had Rita Skeeter been prowling around Hogwarts?

217. Barty Crouch's grandfather had an Axminster flying carpet; how many people could travel on it?

218. Who was head of the delegation from Durmstrang?

219. Whose first name is Olympe?

220. Who asked Angelina Johnson to the Yule Ball?

221. What does a wizard say to discover the last spell that a wand performed?

222. What creatures came to Lord Voldemort in the cemetery after he had risen again?

223. At how many years of age does a unicorn grow its horns?

224. What words did Malfoy's badge display when it was pressed?

225. How much did a pair of Omnioculars cost at the Quidditch World Cup?

226. Who tells Harry that he must get to the Portkey after the connection between his and Lord Voldemort's wands are broken?

227. At which hill is the nearest Portkey to the Weasley's home?

228. Under which teacher does Hermione study when Ron and Harry are taught by Professor Trelawney?

229. What happens to the wailing of the golden egg when Harry puts it under the water?

230. Who was caught smuggling flying carpets into Britain?

231. Who was the first person Harry saw back at Hogwarts after his battle with Lord Voldemort?

232. In what part of Hogwarts did Harry spend the night before the Triwizard Tournament's second task?

233. What do the letters S.P.E.W. stand for?

234. Which captain of a Hogwarts Quidditch team was signed to the Puddlemore United reserve team?

235. What position did Apollyon Pringle hold at Hogwarts when Mrs Weasley was a student there?

236. What mark out of ten did Karkaroff award Harry for his first Triwizard task?

237. How many months did Fred and George Weasley spend developing their Ton-Tongue Toffees?

238. The reverse spell effect is called *Previo Chantum*, *Priori Incantatem*, *Reversi Spellarium* or *Priori Enchantitem*?

239. The pus from which plant is a powerful cure for acne?

240. What sort of dragon did Viktor Krum have to compete against in the first Triwizard task?

241. What is the name of the hospital for magical maladies and injuries?

242. Into which Hogwarts house was Owen Cauldwell sorted?

243. Who told Harry that Karkaroff had been a former Death Eater?

244. What career does Professor Moody suggest Harry should consider?

245. Which former Hogwarts head boy is now working for the Department of International Magical Co-operation?

246. What was the correct answer to the riddle set by the sphinx in the maze?

247. How many giants are left in Britain: hundreds, dozens or none?

248. Which national Quidditch side lost to Transylvania 390 to 10?

249. What is the first obstacle, shaped like a Dementor, which Harry encounters in the maze?

250. Which member of the Ministry of Magic, apart from Mr Crouch, was present at the ceremony to choose the competitors for the Triwizard Tournament?

251. Who manages to gain Harry's golden egg from Professor Snape?

252. Which Hogwarts professor has a brother with the first name Aberforth?

253. Who seemed to perform a Crucio spell on Cedric during the third Triwizard task?

254. When does the selection of the three champions for the Triwizard Tournament take place?

255. Where does Sirius Black meet Harry and Professor Dumbledore?

256. How many years has it been since Britain last hosted the Quidditch World Cup?

257. What creature does Amos Diggory find unconscious in the woods holding a wand?

258. Who only scored 25 points in the second Triwizard Tournament task?

259. How much is Dobby paid a week for working at Hogwarts?

260. Where do Bode and Croaker work: the Department of Mysteries, the Department of Magical Games and Sports or the Department of Muggle History?

261. Who fills in for Mr Crouch as the fifth judge of the Triwizard Tournament's third task?

262. How much does Hermione charge to join S.P.E.W.?

263. Which professor gave Harry permission to practise his impediment jinx and other hexes during lunchtime?

264. Who did Hagrid take to see the four dragons arrive, apart from Harry?

265. What sort of food did Hermione send Harry for the summer holidays?

266. What colour is the serpent found on the Slytherin banner?

267. How many points do Harry and Cedric have before the start of the third Triwizard task?

268. How many Galleons per week did Professor Dumbledore originally offer Dobby?

269. Who brought a Dementor with him to interview Barty Crouch?

270. Which school friend of Harry's insisted that he, Ron and Hermione support the Ireland Quidditch team?

271. How many hands did the Weasley family's clock have?

272. What is the name of the strange mirror Professor Moody uses to check on his enemies?

273. Who does Dumbledore ask to contact Remus Lupin and Arabella Figg?

274. Who used the Accio Summoning Charm to empty Fred and George's pockets of joke sweets?

275. Which Hogwarts student has a father called Frank who was an Auror?

276. How long do all the champions have to complete the second Triwizard task?

277. What spell performed by Ludo Bagman magically magnified his voice so that everyone could hear him?

278. What spell, beginning with the letter I, does Mr Weasley say to start a fire in the Dursleys' fireplace?

279. How many owls carried an entire ham to the mountain where Sirius was living?

280. Who was Ginny Weasley's partner at the Yule Ball?

281. Who beat Peru in the semi-finals of the Quidditch World Cup final?

282. Which one of the following was not among the names of Voldemort's supporters that Karkaroff gave the Ministry: Evan Rosier, Augustus Rookwood, Ivan Relanov?

283. Into which Hogwarts house was Malcolm Baddock sorted?

284. Who did Cho Chang go to the Yule Ball with?

285. Both Harry's and Lord Voldemort's wands have a feather from which creature?

286. Who did Harry see break into Professor Snape's office?

287. Who was the Ravenclaw Quidditch captain: Oliver Wood, Seamus Finnigan or Roger Davies?

288. What password does Harry use to gain entrance to Professor Dumbledore's office?

289. Whose Niffler was the most successful at recovering gold during Hagrid's lesson?

290. Which classmate of Harry's transplanted his own ears onto a cactus?

291. Which two adults does Dumbledore insist put their differences behind them?

292. What sort of creature do Harry, Ron and Hermione see talking to Ludo Bagman in the Three Broomsticks?

293. With what weapon did Wormtail cut off his own hand and cut Harry's arm?

294. What is the name of Fred and George's joke supply business?

295. Which professor gave Harry and Ron weekly essays on the Goblin Rebellions of the eighteenth century?

296. What is the name of the stone basin that holds memories, in Dumbledore's office?

297. What place is to be the site of the third Triwizard Tournament task?

298. What was the name of the Riddles' gardener?

299. Whose mother was called Fridwulfa?

300. What surprising visitor to Hogwarts did Harry spot moving on the Marauders' Map?

Harry Potter and the
Philosopher's Stone Answers

1. A picture card
2. Third
3. Dursley
4. Neville Longbottom
5. A Knut
6. A turban
7. Right-handed
8. A jumper
9. Milk bottles
10. Dungeons

11. A serpent
12. Hogwarts Express
13. Pure gold
14. Eleven
15. Black
16. The smallest
17. In a car crash
18. Over 600
19. Vernon
20. Silver

21. Short
22. A wooden flute
23. Dragon
24. King's Cross
25. Hogwarts
26. The Golden Snitch
27. The Philosopher's Stone
28. Platform nine and
    three-quarters
29. Hagrid
30. Harry's father

31. Slytherin
32. Seven
33. Diagon Alley
34. Gryffindor
35. Lord Voldemort
36. Harry's father
37. Hagrid
38. Filch
39. True
40. His parents

41. A poltergeist
42. The game ends
43. Mr Filch
44. Hermione Granger
45. Nearly Headless Nick
46. Twelve feet
47. Nimbus Two Thousand
48. Neville Longbottom
49. Hermione
50. Destroy it

51. Minus two
52. Green
53. Romania
54. Ron
55. Slytherin
56. Scabbers
57. Three
58. In the cupboard under
    the stairs
59. Professor Snape
60. Bertie Bott

61. Soccer ball
62. Four
63. Centaurs
64. Harry
65. Slytherin
66. Petunia
67. Hufflepuff
68. The Great Hall
69. A broomstick
70. False

71. Red
72. True
73. A dragon
74. Red
75. A ghost
76. The scar on his forehead
77. Wizard chess
78. 1 September
79. Gryffindor
80. Ravenclaw

81. Neville's
82. A pub
83. Four
84. Percy
85. Draco Malfoy
86. Lord Voldemort
87. Hermione
88. Black
89. Silver
90. Seeker

91. Hagrid
92. Hogwarts Express
93. Professor Quirrell
94. Ollivanders
95. Lord Voldemort
96. Illegal
97. Privet Drive
98. The Forbidden Forest
99. Lightning flash
100. Professor Dumbledore

⭐⭐ **Question rating: MEDIUM** ⭐⭐

101. An owl
102. Hermione
103. Dennis, Gordon, Piers and Malcolm
104. The Hog's Head
105. History of Magic
106. Five
107. Pictures of Harry's mother and father
108. Broomsticks
109. A knight
110. Hagrid

111. Professor Snape
112. Lily
113. Twelve
114. Nearly Headless Nick
115. Drink its blood
116. Toad, cat or owl
117. Smeltings
118. Head Boy
119. Silver
120. A Put-Outer

121. Professor Quirrell

122. Diagon Alley
123. 472
124. Dragons
125. Madam Hooch
126. Uncle Vernon
127. Piles of books
128. Hermione
129. Microscope
130. Slytherin

131. A wooden flute
132. 29
133. It was snapped in half
134. Make them immortal
    (live forever)
135. Gringotts
136. A non-magical person
137. Seeker
138. Madam Malkin's
    Robes for all
    Occasions
139. Dudley Dursley
140. Africa

141. 1945
142. Five minutes
143. Twelve
144. In the hospital wing
145. True
146. The book screams
147. James
148. His toad
149. Gryffindor
150. The Leaky Cauldron

151. A pointy wizard's hat
152. Knit

153. The Bloody Baron
154. An Invisibility Cloak
155. Crabbe and Goyle
156. Black
157. 17
158. Eggs
159. 142
160. A tabby cat

161. Fang
162. Diagon Alley
163. Deputy Head
164. Charlie Weasley
165. Hermione
166. Books
167. Lord Voldemort
168. Smeltings
169. Gryffindor
170. Hagrid

171. Professor Dumbledore
172. Gringott's Bank
173. Wizard chess
174. None
175. A memory aid
176. Nicolas Flamel
177. Ten pin bowling
178. Charlie Weasley's
179. Piers Polkiss
180. Charms

181. The girls' toilets
182. Percy Weasley
183. Walnut
184. Mrs Figg
185. Chamber music
186. Firenze

187. Gold
188. Professor Dumbledore
189. A rifle
190. 50

191. Fred and George
192. The *Daily Prophet*
193. A club

194. Three
195. Seven
196. Chocolate
197. Bludgers
198. False
199. Weasley
200. The Seeker

⭐⭐⭐ Question rating: HARD ⭐⭐⭐

201. 60
202. Six
203. A giant squid
204. Leg-locking curse
205. Maroon
206. A pineapple
207. Albus
208. Five
209. Draco Malfoy
210. Mahogany

211. Professor Snape
212. Makes them fly
213. Football
214. Hagrid
215. 700
216. Harry's father
217. London Underground
218. Neville
219. Devon
220. A pig's tail

221. 112%
222. Seven
223. Draco Malfoy

224. A toilet seat
225. Madam Hooch
226. Grunnings
227. Just in case
228. Professor Sprout
229. Draco Malfoy
230. A coat hanger or a pair of Uncle Vernon's old socks

231. Professor McGonagall's
232. The broomshed
233. Harry's
234. Cornelius Fudge
235. Devil's Snare
236. Mrs Figg
237. An Anti-Cheating spell
238. A boa constrictor
239. Send up green sparks with their wands
240. The three-headed dog

241. Professor McGonagall
242. Drills

243. The Forbidden Forest
244. Professor McGonagall
245. Norwegian Ridgeback
246. Sirius Black
247. Dentistry
248. Professor Snape
249. The Ministry of Magic
250. Minerva

251. Four
252. 24
253. Fluffy
254. November
255. A centaur
256. The Bloody Baron
257. The Mirror of Erised
258. The thing that they most want
259. Chicken's blood
260. Its own club

261. Stonewall High
262. Beaters
263. Blue
264. Potions
265. Himself holding a pair of socks
266. Goblins
267. Filch
268. Goat
269. The horn and the tail hair
270. A fifty pence piece

271. Ron
272. Mahogany
273. Norbert
274. Severus
275. A teddy bear
276. Earwax
277. Crabbe
278. Draco Malfoy and Neville
279. Slytherin
280. Potter for President

281. A troll
282. Seamus Finnigan
283. History of Magic
284. Knuts
285. Himself
286. Lee Jordan
287. Glass
288. Gryffindor house
289. The library (the Restricted Section)
290. Professor Dumbledore

291. Ten
292. 11o'clock at night
293. Oliver Wood
294. Willow
295. Broken wrist
296. Railview Hotel
297. Midnight
298. Professor Snape
299. Seamus Finnigan
300. Transfiguration

Harry Potter and the
Chamber of Secrets Answers

Question rating: EASY

1. A dwarf
2. The Whomping Willow
3. Gilderoy Lockhart
4. Gryffindor
5. Six
6. Lucius Malfoy
7. Slytherin
8. Moaning Myrtle
9. His pet owl
10. Ginny

11. Over 1000 years ago
12. Outside school
13. Salazar Slytherin
14. Ron Weasley
15. Two
16. Jokes
17. A witch
18. A monster
19. Mudblood
20. Madam Pince

21. Harry
22. A milkman
23. True
24. Hogwarts
25. His arm
26. Ron Weasley
27. Several weeks
28. Salazar Slytherin
29. They were cancelled
30. Slytherin

31. In the cupboard under
    the stairs
32. Four
33. Nearly Headless Nick
34. Black
35. Pinhead
36. Nearly Headless Nick
37. Gilderoy Lockhart
38. 50
39. Spiders
40. A house-elf

41. Afternoon
42. Moaning Myrtle
43. Third year
44. Ginny
45. Hedwig
46. The Weasleys
47. Floo powder
48. Harry
49. A living witch
50. Nothing

51. A cat hair
52. A tree
53. False
54. Ginny Weasley
55. The *Evening Prophet*
56. Professor McGonagall
57. Gryffindor and Slytherin
58. Harry
59. Hufflepuff
60. Mandrake

61. A prefect
62. Gryffindor
63. The Ministry of Magic
64. Gryffindor
65. Azkaban
66. True
67. Ron
68. The Bludgers
69. The Easter Holidays
70. A hairpin

71. True
72. Percy Weasley
73. Black
74. The Weasleys' car
75. Draco Malfoy
76. Gilderoy Lockhart
77. The Weasleys'
78. Valentines Day
79. Gilderoy Lockhart
80. Hagrid

81. Ginny Weasley
82. A Muggle
83. Chaser
84. Ordinary Wizarding Levels
85. The Invisibility Cloak
86. Gryffindor
87. Yes
88. Dobby
89. His wand
90. Moaning Myrtle

91. In his bedroom
92. Dumbledore
93. A lake
94. Hermione
95. Twelve
96. Fred and George Weasley
97. Tom Riddle
98. A silver sword
99. A ghoul
100. Hermione

101. Fifth-year
102. Moaning Myrtle
103. Chamber of Secrets
104. Improper Use of Magic Office
105. The girls' toilets
106. 500
107. Ginny Weasley
108. Defence Against the Dark Arts
109. T.M. Riddle

110. Mr Weasley and Mr Malfoy

111. Harry's
112. Goyle's
113. A giant spider
114. Lockhart
115. Turquoise
116. Muggle Studies
117. Lucius Malfoy
118. A cat flap

119. The Bludger
120. Draco Malfoy

121. Harry
122. Elbow
123. Wattlebird
124. One hour
125. Salazar Slytherin
126. A stool
127. Moaning Myrtle
128. Spiders
129. Dobby
130. Polyjuice Potion

131. Slugs
132. Emeralds
133. Signed copies of
     one of his books
     (*Magical Me*)
134. Goyle
135. Miranda Goshawk
136. North
137. Through the
     blackboard
138. Draco Malfoy
139. Dobby
140. A barn owl

141. It became covered in
     black fur
142. The Sorting Hat
143. Grey
144. A crossbow
145. Knockturn Alley
146. Harry
147. Red
148. Fawkes

149. A Basilisk
150. A gnome

151. Draco Malfoy's
152. Kwikspell
153. Ron and Harry
154. True
155. Professor
     Dumbledore's
156. Owls
157. A Bludger
158. None
159. Mrs Norris the cat
160. Draco Malfoy

161. Shooting Star
162. Harry
163. Arthur
164. Gilderoy Lockhart's
165. Their car
166. Colin Creevey
167. Hermione
168. A tickling charm
169. Professor Lockhart
170. Mr Weasley

171. Dobby
172. Draco Malfoy
173. Red
174. Marvolo
175. His glasses
176. Lockhart and Snape
177. Hufflepuff
178. False
179. A piece of paper
180. McGonagall

181. The *Daily Prophet*
182. Nearly Headless Nick
183. None
184. Basilisk
185. A large quill
186. Flourish and Blotts
187. Elephant
188. He padlocked it
189. Goyle and Crabbe
190. The Whomping Willow

191. Spiders
192. The Chudley Cannons
193. Lockhart
194. A new broomstick
195. His finger
196. Fawkes the phoenix
197. A toothpick
198. Cornish pixies
199. Percy Weasley
200. Swelling Solution

★★★ Question rating: HARD ★★★

201. Tom Riddle's diary
202. De-gnome the garden
203. Skele-Gro
204. Godric Gryffindor's
205. Professor Dippet
206. 45
207. The pudding
208. Inside a wardrobe
209. Twelve
210. It was cancelled

211. Ford Anglia
212. A rooster
213. Lockhart
214. Phoenix tears
215. Ravenclaw
216. Dumbledore and McGonagall
217. The Burrow
218. Peeves
219. Lucius Malfoy
220. 200

221. Astronomy
222. Mason
223. Earmuffs
224. The murder of a girl
225. Bicorn horn
226. It lost all of its bones
227. Five
228. Colin Creevey
229. Sixteen
230. The Chudley Cannons

231. Mr Filch
232. Defence Against the Dark Arts
233. A tin of treacle fudge
234. Nimbus two thousand and one
235. Neville Longbottom
236. His sock
237. Filch
238. 50
239. Two green eyes
240. Memory charms

241. In an armchair in front of the staff-room fire
242. Molly
243. Justin Finch-Fletchley
244. Professor McGonagall
245. Cornish pixies
246. Chocolate cakes
247. Armando
248. Rowena
249. *Magical Me*
250. Pure-blood

251. Lucius Malfoy
252. Peeves
253. A Squib
254. Five years
255. Hermione
256. Parselmouth
257. Pepperup Potion
258. Fang
259. Millicent Bulstrode's
260. Mandrake

261. One
262. Seeker
263. Cornelius Fudge
264. Its mouth
265. Yellow
266. Godric
267. Fireworks
268. The Sorting Hat
269. McGonagall
270. In limericks

271. *Lumos*
272. Draco Malfoy
273. A mirror
274. 46
275. A Basilisk
276. *Serpensortia*
277. Slytherin's true heir
278. It bursts into flames
279. Ernie Macmillan
280. Draco Malfoy's

281. Salazar Slytherin
282. Professor Snape's
283. Herbology
284. 150
285. Percy Weasley
286. Three feet
287. Hagrid's
288. Parseltongue
289. Seamus Finnigan
290. Borgin and Burkes

291. *Most Potente Potions*
292. 'I am Lord Voldemort'
293. Tom
294. Marcus Flint
295. Orange
296. She has been Petrified
297. Professor Snape
298. Head Hockey
299. Hermione's
300. Birds

Harry Potter and the
Prisoner of Azkaban Answers

1. A werewolf
2. Hogsmeade
3. Peeves
4. Divination
5. The Shrieking Shack
6. *Which Broomstick?*
7. Percy Weasley
8. Twelve
9. Astronomy
10. The Fat Lady

11. A Time-Turner
12. Gryffindor
13. Hufflepuff
14. Vernon Dursley
15. Cedric Diggory
16. A broomstick
17. The Knight Bus
18. Slytherin
19. Hagrid
20. Sweets

21. He turned into a werewolf
22. Professor McGonagall
23. True
24. Professor Snape
25. Sirius Black
26. The Three Broomsticks
27. Scabbers
28. The Leaky Cauldron
29. Professor Lupin
30. Gryffindor

31. Owls
32. Professor McGonagall
33. Professor Lupin
34. Seventh floor
35. Professor Snape
36. The Quidditch World Cup
37. Purple
38. Azkaban
39. Potions
40. Sirius Black

41. The Post Office
42. Defence Against the Dark Arts
43. Open a window
44. Peter Pettigrew
45. On the day they finish their exams
46. In water
47. Three
48. Sirius Black
49. She swelled so that she was completely round
50. A banshee

51. Hogsmeade
52. The Whomping Willow
53. Sirius Black
54. A Boggart
55. In Hogsmeade
56. Professor Lupin
57. A new wand

58. Professor Dumbledore
59. A dog
60. Sirius Black

61. False
62. France
63. A broken leg
64. True
65. Peter Pettigrew
66. Dementors
67. Hedwig
68. Neville
69. Ron Weasley
70. A cat

71. Hermione and Ron
72. The Leaky Cauldron
73. Divination
74. True
75. A broomstick
76. The Three Broomsticks
77. Divination
78. Fourth-year
79. Tom
80. Water demon

81. Gryffindor
82. London
83. The Fat Lady
84. False
85. Gryffindor
86. The Firebolt
87. Harry
88. False
89. Beds
90. Care of Magical Creatures

91. Ginger
92. Sirius Black or Peter Pettigrew
93. Draco Malfoy
94. Hermione
95. Harry
96. Harry's
97. Sirius Black
98. Wendelin the Weird
99. Ron's
100. Hogsmeade

⭐⭐ **Question rating: MEDIUM** ⭐⭐

101. Turn into an animal
102. A bow
103. Executioner
104. Oliver Wood
105. Professor Lupin
106. Poppy
107. Hermione
108. Gobstones
109. A Time-Turner

110. Ron Weasley

111. A Grindylow
112. The Slytherin v Gryffindor Quidditch match
113. Bill Weasley
114. A Boggart
115. A Dementor

116. True
117. Sirius Black
118. Draco Malfoy
119. James Potter (Harry's father)
120. A holiday to Egypt

121. Neville Longbottom
122. A wand
123. Professor Lupin
124. Harry's
125. Cho Chang
126. Wales
127. Professor Snape
128. Hippogriff
129. Draco Malfoy's
130. Aunt Marge

131. Sirius Black
132. Ripper
133. Professor Lupin
134. The Marauder's Map
135. Sundaes
136. Honeydukes
137. Professor Lupin
138. A broom cloth
139. A toe
140. Professor McGonagall

141. Buckbeak the Hippogriff
142. Two months
143. Sir Cadogan
144. Peter Pettigrew
145. Divination
146. The Dementors
147. An ice-cream parlour

148. Red Caps
149. True
150. Defence Against the Dark Arts

151. Harry's
152. Slytherin
153. 50 feet
154. Cho Chang
155. Crookshanks
156. James Potter (Harry's father)
157. A Broomstick Servicing Kit
158. Sirius Black
159. Liquid was squirted into their face
160. The portrait of the Fat Lady

161. None
162. Last day
163. Three
164. False
165. Hagrid
166. Sirius Black
167. *Unfogging the Future*
168. A giant black dog
169. A shield between a person and a Dementor
170. Green

171. Percy Weasley
172. Professor Dumbledore
173. Chocolate

174. Care of Magical
     Creatures
175. Yes
176. Harry
177. Intermediate
     Transfiguration
178. Dementors
179. Professor Trelawney
180. A Dementor

181. Wormhead
182. An ice-cream parlour
183. Percy Weasley
184. Pocket Sneakoscope
185. Ron
186. Ron

187. Hermione
188. Seven
189. Bighead Boy
190. False

191. Tea leaves
192. Crookshanks
193. Conductor on
     the Knight Bus
194. Two
195. Aunt Petunia
196. Flobberworms
197. Hagrid
198. Professor Dumbledore
199. Bulldogs
200. Chocolate

⭐⭐⭐ Question rating: HARD ⭐⭐⭐

201. 320%
202. Professor Lupin
203. Sirius Black
204. R.J.
205. *Riddikulus*
206. Wendelin the Weird
207. Charms
208. Seven
209. Neville's pet toad
210. Crookshanks

211. September
212. Hagrid
213. Wolfsbane Potion
214. A Pocket Sneakoscope
215. Join the Ministry
     of Magic
216. Cedric Diggory

217. A belt
218. Mrs Weasley
219. Hippogriffs
220. Charlie Weasley

221. Four
222. Neville
223. They crashed into
     each other
224. Stroke the spine with
     your finger
225. Sirius Black
226. Errol
227. Three
228. Care of Magical
     Creatures
229. Marcus Flint
230. Lucius Malfoy

231. Ron Weasley
232. Easter
233. Hagrid's cabin
234. 700
235. Professor Snape
236. Twice
237. The Marauder's Map
238. A vulture
239. Ernie Prang
240. Seven

241. Fifth year
242. Fourteen inches
243. Muggle Studies
244. Under a loose floorboard
245. Three
246. Professor Trelawney
247. Accidental Magic Reversal Department
248. Peeves
249. The Whomping Willow
250. Arthur Weasley

251. Professor Snape
252. Professor Flitwick
253. Vincent
254. Professor Snape
255. Ten
256. Cornelius Fudge
257. Five
258. Kappas
259. A stag
260. In the Great Hall

261. Sir Cadogan

262. Neville Longbottom
263. Padfoot
264. Bathilda Bagshot
265. 711
266. Twelve
267. His finger
268. Eleven
269. 'Mischief managed'
270. Himself

271. Cornelius Fudge
272. Professor Lupin and Ron
273. Twelve
274. A tortoise
275. Lavender Brown's
276. Hot chocolate
277. Professor Trelawney
278. Neville Longbottom
279. The staff room
280. Fred and George Weasley

281. Hermione
282. Dean Thomas
283. Cho Chang
284. Magnolia Crescent
285. 100
286. Oliver Wood
287. Twelve
288. Dog biscuits
289. Cornelius Fudge
290. 50

291. Harry's Invisibility Cloak
292. Five

293. Hinkypunk
294. Thirteen
295. Professor McGonagall
296. The Weasleys'

297. Werewolves
298. *Nox*
299. Peeves'
300. A television

Harry Potter and the Goblet of Fire Answers

1. Three
2. Hermione
3. The *Daily Prophet*
4. Viktor Krum
5. Dudley Dursley
6. Eagle
7. Moaning Myrtle
8. Water
9. Beauxbatons
10. Ron Weasley

11. Mother
12. Ireland
13. Hagrid's
14. Viktor Krum
15. An egg
16. It vanishes
17. Winky
18. Fleur Delacour
19. Merpeople
20. Green

21. Diggory
22. Professor Trelawney
23. The Weird Sisters
24. Twelve feet
25. Wormtail
26. Gold
27. A joke shop
28. The Goblet of Fire
29. Giants
30. Mrs Weasley

31. A tea-cosy
32. Five
33. Hagrid
34. 100,000
35. Ludo Bagman
36. Vernon Dursley
37. Her teeth
38. Madame Maxime
39. False
40. True

41. Harry
42. Bill Weasley
43. Canary Creams
44. Wimbourne Wasps
45. True
46. A giant spider
47. Professor Moody
48. Igor
49. His broomstick
50. One year

51. Three
52. February
53. Lord Voldemort
54. Crouch
55. True
56. Rita Skeeter
57. Sirius Black
58. Fred and George Weasley
59. True
60. Moody

61. Purple
62. October
63. Hermione
64. Viktor Krum
65. Bulgaria
66. Exams
67. Professor Moody
68. Hermione
69. Omnioculars
70. Madame Maxime

71. At Hogwarts
72. A Portkey
73. Last
74. Cedric Diggory
75. Red
76. Ireland
77. 20 feet high
78. Death Eaters
79. Ron
80. Harry

81. Durmstrang
82. Lord Voldemort
83. A unicorn
84. True
85. Thirteen
86. Dobby
87. Cornelius Fudge
88. One Galleon
89. Emerald green
90. Gold

91. Wood
92. Bulgaria
93. 1000
94. Cho Chang
95. Harry's
96. Mrs Weasley
97. June
98. Viktor Krum
99. Hermione
100. July

⭐⭐ **Question rating: MEDIUM** ⭐⭐

101. Hufflepuff
102. Apparating
103. Harry
104. Professor Snape
105. 43
106. Sixteen
107. Draco Malfoy
108. A shark
109. The Yule Ball
110. One week

111. True
112. Ten

113. One year
114. Cho Chang
115. Monday
116. Mrs Weasley and Bill Weasley
117. Professor Sprout
118. Merpeople
119. False
120. 20 feet

121. Professor Moody
122. Tropical birds
123. Cedric Diggory

124. Viktor Krum
125. Four
126. Ludo Bagman
127. Crouch
128. Blue
129. Lord Voldemort
130. It explodes

131. Ron Weasley
132. Latvian Long-Snout
133. Troy
134. Dennis
135. Fawkes
136. Thursday
137. Harry
138. Sirius Black
139. A badger
140. Uganda

141. Lord Voldemort
142. Professor Sprout
143. Niffler
144. Draco Malfoy
145. Beauxbatons
146. A musical group
147. True
148. A chicken
149. The Hanged Man
150. Moaning Myrtle

151. Eighteen
152. Lucius Malfoy
153. Mr Roberts
154. Professor Snape
155. A spider
156. Professor Snape
157. Mundungus Fletcher

158. Ten feet
159. The Chudley Cannons
160. Professor Trelawney

161. Ton-Tongue Toffee
162. Hermione
163. Seventeen
164. Ludo Bagman
165. Hagrid
166. Professor Moody
167. Over 700 years ago
168. False
169. Goblin Liaison Office
170. Gobbledygook

171. Hedwig
172. Snuffles
173. Socks
174. Auror
175. The Triwizard Cup
176. Beater
177. Durmstrang
178. Peeves
179. Ginny Weasley
180. Professor Dumbledore

181. Cedric Diggory
182. The Quidditch Cup
183. Fleur Delacour
184. Denis Creevey
185. Veelas
186. Madame Maxime
187. Cedric Diggory
188. Ron Weasley
189. Blue
190. A Quidditch
     foul

191. Professor Moody
192. False
193. Egyptian
194. Mr Ollivander
195. Cornelius Fudge

196. Three
197. Maroon
198. Harry
199. Albania
200. Fleur Delacour

⭐⭐⭐ Question rating: HARD ⭐⭐⭐

201. Cedric Diggory
202. Splinch
203. Wizarding Wireless Network
204. One
205. Tell the truth
206. An Ageing Potion
207. Little Hangleton
208. A Bludger
209. Hassan Mustafa
210. Tom Riddle

211. Pine-fresh
212. Two
213. Dobby and Winky
214. *Witch Weekly*
215. 437
216. A beetle
217. Twelve
218. Professor Karkaroff
219. Madame Maxime
220. Fred Weasley

221. *Prior Incantato*
222. Death Eaters
223. Four
224. Potter Stinks
225. Ten Galleons

226. James Potter (Harry's dad)
227. Stoatshead Hill
228. Professor Vector
229. It turns into a chorus of singing
230. Ali Bashir

231. Professor Dumbledore
232. The library
233. Society for the Protection of Elfish Welfare
234. Oliver Wood
235. Caretaker
236. Four
237. Six
238. *Priori Incantatem*
239. Bubotuber
240. Chinese Fireball

241. St Mungo's Hospital
242. Hufflepuff
243. Sirius Black
244. Being an Auror
245. Percy Weasley
246. Spider
247. None

248. England
249. A Boggart
250. Ludo Bagman

251. Professor Moody
252. Professor Dumbledore
253. Viktor Krum
254. Hallowe'en
255. In Dumbledore's office
256. 30 years
257. Winky the house-elf
258. Fleur Delacour
259. One Galleon
260. Department of Mysteries

261. Cornelius Fudge
262. Two sickles
263. Professor McGonagall
264. Madame Maxime
265. Sugar-free sweets
266. Silver
267. 85 points
268. Ten
269. Cornelius Fudge
270. Seamus Finnigan

271. Nine
272. A Foe-Glass
273. Sirius Black
274. Mrs Weasley

275. Neville Longbottom
276. One hour
277. *Sonorus*
278. *Incendio*
279. Three
280. Neville Longbottom

281. Ireland
282. Ivan Relanov
283. Slytherin
284. Cedric Diggory
285. Fawkes the phoenix
286. Mr Crouch
287. Roger Davies
288. Cockroach Cluster
289. Ron's
290. Neville Longbottom

291. Sirius Black and Professor Snape
292. Goblins
293. A silver dagger
294. *Weasleys' Wizard Wheezes*
295. Professor Binns
296. The Pensieve
297. The Quidditch pitch
298. Frank Bryce
299. Hagrid's
300. Mr Crouch